Social Media Marketing
2020

How to Crush it With Instagram Marketing

Proven Strategies to Build Your Brand, Reach Millions of Customers, and Grow Your Business Without Wasting Time and Money

Social Media Marketing 2020

Your Free Gift

As a way of saying thanks for your purchase, I wanted to offer you two free bonuses - *"**The Fastest Way to Make Money with Affiliate Marketing**"* and *"*Top 10 **Affiliate Offers to Promote**"* cheat sheets, exclusive to the readers of this book.

To get instant access just or go to:

https://theartofmastery.com/chandler-free-gift

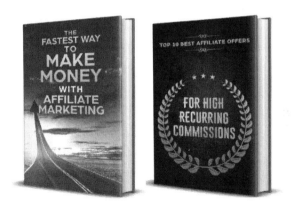

Inside the cheat sheets, you will discover:

- The fastest way to start generating income with affiliate marketing

- My top 10 favorite affiliate offers to promote for high recurring commissions
- Access to a FREE live training where you will learn:
- how one affiliate marketer built a $500,000 a month business all while traveling the world...
- The 3-step system to eliminate risk and instability in your online business
- The 7 biggest mistakes affiliates make in making money online
- How tech companies are giving away FREE MONEY to help you start
- And much more...

Once again, to get instant access just go to:

https://theartofmastery.com/chandler-free-gift

Table of Contents

YOUR FREE GIFT 3

INTRODUCTION 6

CHAPTER 1. INSTAGRAM: AN INTRODUCTION . 9

CHAPTER 2: THE CONTENT CREATION
PROCESS 27

CHAPTER 3: THE POWER OF IMAGES 49

CHAPTER 4: UNDERSTANDING YOUR
INSTAGRAM AUDIENCE 66

CHAPTER 5: USING INSTAGRAM STORIES TO
BUILD YOUR BRAND 95

CHAPTER 6: SHOPPING IN INSTAGRAM 114

CHAPTER 7: APPEALING TO GENERATION Z .. 131

CHAPTER 8: PUBLIC RELATIONS ON
INSTAGRAM 151

CHAPTER 9: REACHING THE ONLINE
MARKETING PLATEAU 163

CONCLUSION 176

THANK YOU 181

Introduction

The goal of marketing has always been to push target audience members into making a conscious choice to purchase a product, subscribe to a service, or to even change their perspective on a certain issue or topic. As such, we cannot rally fault old-time marketing strategies in being pushy with their messaging. After all, how else are you going to do something if it is not hammered to your head that whatever they want you to do is of great importance?

But here is the problem with the market today: *Things Have Changed.*

With the dawn of the Age of the Internet, a stronger focus has been put on consumer agency and choice. Now, the consumer is less of a drone who is susceptible to overt coercion to do or purchase something and more of a thinking buyer who puts a lot of thought and care into every purchasing decision they make.

There is also fact that the Internet right now is divided into many communities, each with their own language, culture, and overall philosophy.

A person who uses Facebook tends to display certain expected behaviors while using the site and another who frequents YouTube will do so differently at that platform.

The point is that marketers need to know how people think and feel on each known site in order to craft a message that they will respond positively when exposed to. This is where Instagram comes into play as it is one of the easiest platforms to overlook, underestimate, and disregard as marketing tool.

What many are not aware of is that the platform can actually be used to expand the reach of any brand for a fraction of the cost and effort one typically spends in other social media sites.

Think of it this way: imagine that you are an experienced baseball player who suddenly has to make a career shift into cricket. The two ball games might be different but the skills you learned in the former will still be essential in the latter.

This is the same when venturing into a new kind of platform for marketing such as Instagram. The rules might be different there but the concepts that bind the whole thing together are the same.

To put it in other words, survival and success in your venture into Instagram depend greatly on your ability to adapt to the culture there without forgetting about the basics of online marketing.

The only question, however, is *how you are supposed to do that.* In this book, you will go through the different conceptual differences that make Instagram stand out as a platform and a viable marketing channel. You will also learn how to craft your message there and create content that will get that message across to your target audience.

Of course, you will also be acquainted with the most successful brands on the site right now and how they managed to establish themselves in it.

Just do remember that Instagram is just like any other site out there. You have to know what makes it tick in order to make your stay there as successful and profitable as possible. If done right, you might just be on your way to creating marketing campaigns that will definitely turn heads on the platform – and for the right reasons, of course.

Chapter 1. Instagram: An Introduction

So what makes Instagram, well, different?

The most basic description of Instagram is that is an image sharing platform in the vein of older forums like 4Chan and 9gag. However, the way it presents its content can be seen as something a bit more elaborate or, for the lack of any other word, flashy.

But as for the viability of the platform as a marketing channel, there are a few facts about the site that you need to be aware of.

User Population

Instagram has over a billion active users (which are users who have logged in in the past month. Over 60% of these people login on a daily basis. Half of the user population follow brands.

80% of its population is comprised of private individuals while the rest is are small time businesses, large corporations, non-profit organizations, and any other entity made by laws and incorporation.

The biggest segment that makes up Instagram's entire population belongs to the Teenager Young Adult crowd. These are people aged 14 to 30 and have one of the most active spending behavior in the Internet in recent years.

In addition, 32 of teens in the US reported that this platform is the most important social network for them.

Frequency

An estimate of 51% of Instagram's users log in to their accounts at least once per day. Also, 37.5% of these users use Instagram's Stories feature on a daily basis while a third of the population come from businesses.

Also, visual content in the form of photos happened to be the most engaged type of content in the site at 58%. Aside from that, images that pertain to Fashion, Lifestyle, and Inspiration tend to be consumed the most.

As for peak engagement at the site, it spans at 4 to 5pm, regardless of the time zone. This means that there could always be a spike in Instagram activity at any time in any place across the world.

Other Metrics

Surprisingly, people tend to consume Instagram photos with the least bit amount of edits and filtering. This means that there is no popular photo type or filter that Instagram users prefer sharing and engaging at the site.

As far as advertising is concerned, the site is home to more than 2 million advertisements and other marketing campaigns on a monthly basis. For profiles, they have the potential to gather no less than 600 followers in their lifetime while also being connected to an average of 350 active accounts.

All in all, these data shows that Instagram makes for a rather robust network and a fairly effective marketing tool to add to your list of online marketing channels.

Unique Features

But what exactly makes Instagram unique? Generally speaking, Instagram offers three unique features that no other site has replicated yet.

1. Mobile Optimization from the Ground Up

Technically speaking, Instagram is not mobile optimized. However, this is only so as the phrase "mobile optimization" connotes that the site was made to adapt to mobile devices as far as their screen sizes and navigation systems are concerned. The truth is that Instagram has been designed for mobile users right from the very start.

This is quite important as mobile users already take up a third of the world's population of Internet users in recent years. In Instagram, everything from content creation to marketing can be down in one hand. If connected to the right accounts, a single person can be exposed to a near-infinite scroll of new content every time that they are logged in to the site.

2. A Highly Visual Medium

As will be discussed later on, visuals happen to be a fairly effective medium with which to do your marketing. The impact that they can generate with a fraction of the effort needed to set up other marketing mediums is something that no marketer should ever underestimate.

Fortunately, Instagram is a platform that encourages that use of visual media. In fact, the most engaged kind of content on the site right now are pictures and the best ones tend to net in comments, shares, and likes by the hundreds of thousands to even millions. That is the kind of engagement that one cannot purchase through paid advertising.

Also, Instagram can automatically adjust the sizing of photos so that they are uniform on the platform. This way, your marketing campaigns can look coherent and do not break immersion from one image to another.

3. Simplicity

However, what gives Instagram its strong staying power in recent years is the sheer simplicity of using it. Its interface is not as cumbersome as the ones found in, say, YouTube or Facebook which makes it a hit for younger demographics. For marketers, this means that they can also easily monitor the engagements for their content without having to sift through pages of charts and readings.

Also, the simplicity of the site means that businesses can leverage their presence without having to understand the more technical and finnicky stuff that runs the entire platform. Lastly, the community on the site right now has an energy and willingness to consume all kinds of content that no other site has managed to compete with.

4. Re-Using Content

In some ways, Instagram provides marketers with the ability to repurpose their content. You have a long article that you want to share on Instagram? Turn it into an infographic. If you have a video on YouTube, take a memorable still from that and post it on the platform.

The point is that even old marketing campaigns can find a place on Instagram and still be effective in funneling traffic there. This should save you a lot of time from having to plan content specifically for the platform.

5. Cross-Channel Marketing

More often than not, Instagram can make for a perfect fit to your already existing marketing campaigns. In fact, by adding one more site to your list marketing channels, you can increase the amount of traffic to your site and expand the reach of your brand in new markets.

For example, you may display your Instagram photos on your website. When a customer browses through the site, there is a chance that they may not have been following your Instagram profile.

But if they see a link to your gallery in Instagram at your own site, they would click to see your account, start following you, and get a constant stream of new content from it every time they log in to their own IG account.

Alternatively, a follower on Instagram might not have known of your site. With the Shoppable Instagram version, they can go to the shop version of your IG account, click through the products on offer there and be taken to your website.

Either way, Instagram provides another point of entry for potential customers in learning more about your business. And, aside from that, they can get to know your business more from every site that your account can take them to.

Some Caveats

So, marketing in Instagram should be easy with all these advantages, right?

Wrong.

Just as with any other website out there, Instagram has a few quirks that make it far from the perfect social media platform to market in.

1. Linking is Next to Impossible

Unless you include them on your main profile or creatively include them in each post, you cannot directly include links to outside pages for your marketing campaigns on the website. The reason for this is that Instagram wants to discourage businesses from flooding their target audience's feed with their content and maintain a balance between user-generated and promotional content.

However, as was stated, there is a way to include links to your marketing content. You only have to do so in a way that is not as direct and blatant as in other social media sites.

2. Text Content is Near Ineffective

Instagram, as a highly visual medium, is not exactly the best place to do purely text-based marketing. People come to Instagram for cool and inspirational images that they can share in other sites. This means that you have to master the art of delivering your marketing message using only a few words or a few short sentences. If you have to use text in your content, you have to find a way to incorporate it in more engaging forms of media in order to gain some traction for your campaigns.

3. No Conversations

Again due to the fact that Instagram is a highly visual medium, starting a direct conversation with your target audience and customers in the site is rather difficult, if not impossible. The platform just wasn't designed for that.

If that is the main concept behind your marketing campaigns, it is best that you adjust to the limitations of Instagram so that you can still generate engagements for your brand. If not, then you might have to use those marketing campaigns for other platforms.

Native Advertising: What is It and How Can You Use It?

The goal of content marketing in any social media site has always been rather simple: go to where people congregate and then provide them with something that they are looking for (or, at the very least, are aware of). If they like what you have to offer, then engagement with your brand will increase.

However, there is one term that content marketers have been using frequent in recent years and it is called Native Advertising. In more ways than one, this is what should help you establish your foothold in Instagram given its rather unique concept. Or, generally speaking, it should help you improve the way you push your content in any social media platform that you wish to operate on.

1. What is It?

In the simplest terms possible, native advertising is simply the marketing strategies that you use that is native to the platform that you promote on. To make this easier for you, let's have an example:

In Instagram, the most engaged kind of content are images and the most popular theme are Fashion, Lifestyle, and Inspiration. As such, native advertising for Instagram involves the use of images that are aimed to brighten one's mood or uplift their spirits. For Twitter, the native form of advertising will be Tweets. For YouTube, that would be videos. And so and so forth.

2. Why Should You Use It?

As with any other marketing strategy out there, the reason you should be considering using native advertising in Instagram is for the advantages that it offers. Here are some of them:

a. Increased Brand Awareness

If you produce content that is native to the platform you are advertising on, you can attract the attention of your audience at a more efficient rate. You have to consider that performance metrics are essential to your campaigns as they can immediately tell you if your strategies are working in real time.

In this regard, native advertising, tends to offer better engagement rates, quicker conversions, and a generally higher level of brand awareness and loyalty. As an added bonus, the chances of audiences creating their own marketing efforts such as comments, shares, reviews, and testimonials for you is higher if you shift to native advertising.

b. Better Content Relevance

If you produce content that is compatible to Instagram, especially in the language it uses and through the tools that the site offers, it would be easier for your audience to share and engage with it. You have to remember that the best kind of advertising is those that encourage trust and loyalty in the brand.

As such, creating content that not only fits the format but also the culture of Instagram, makes any topic that you raise or any solution you propose through your marketing all the more consumable. If there's plenty of engagement, there is even a chance that your content is going to become viral. And that is always something that a lot of online marketers would prefer.

c. Customer Agency

The updates in Google's algorithms have shown that customer behavior in recent years have shifted from a fact-finding approach to a more problem-solving orientation. In essence, they just don't find stuff online for knowledge's sake. They need to find ways to make that knowledge applicable in practical and real-world scenarios.

Native advertising, in this regard, helps marketers push content that provides value to their audiences. The core concept of the strategy is not to only present ideas and themes that would make people convert into customers but to present such in a manner that relates to them on a personal level and gives a solution to a problem that they constantly deal with.

For instance, you might be a seller of countertops and you use your IG profile to showcase what you offer to the market. If you are only showing good countertops without even an explanation why or just for purely marketing purposes, you are not going to attain a lot of traction on the site.

However, if you present your offerings by showcasing them as part of a lifestyle or even highlight some eco-friendly options here and there, you are at the very least tapping into a need that people have in relation to the kind of products that you are offering. After all, who does not want a countertop today that is nice to look at, durable, germ-resistant, and made with environmentally conscious materials?

Simply put, native advertising can help you convince your audience that you may be in the market not only for profit but also to offering something that is valuable, real, and sustainable. If you show that you care more than the money that you could earn from these people, your audiences would tend to reward you more with their loyalty.

Setting Up Your Instagram Account

Getting your own Instagram account activated is a fairly straightforward process. In fact, you can do this within a few short minutes if you want to.

Step 1. Download the App

Although the desktop version can be accessed through an Internet Browser and integrates well with your existing PC setup, the mobile version would actually play a more crucial role for your marketing.

With the app, you can immediately publish any image that you have taken and interact with your audiences on the go. It would really help you do your Instagram marketing while you are doing other tasks.

Step 2. Sign Up

Of course, you'd have to let Instagram know who you are by filling up an information sheet. This includes your name (or the business's name), e-mail address, other basic information like age, gender, and physical address, and your password.

Alternatively, since Instagram is linked with Facebook, you can choose to log in with your Facebook account which duplicates all your basic information from the latter to the former.

Step 3. Switch to a Business Account

Within Instagram's setting is an option that says Switch to Business Profile. This is a rather crucial step to take as Business Profiles have some inherent advantages over normal profiles which would really help you in your marketing campaigns.

In fact, here are some of the advantages that you could expect if you set up a Business Profile.

- **Advanced Analytics**

  Instagram will provide you real-time data to help you determine whether or not your marketing campaign was successful there. It will tally up any kind of engagement your content gets from likes, shares, and comments and then present them in a format that is easy to process and interpret.

- **Extra Business Information**

  With a business profile, you have the added advantage of letting your audience know other pertinent business information like the physical address, store hours, main webpage, and other contact information.

Remember that although online marketing is needed, it is on-foot traffic (where people actually show up to your business to make a transaction) where things matter the most. You have to let people know where you are setting up shop so they can part with their money as soon as they are converted.

- **Marked for Marketing**

  With a business profile, every content you published is immediately tagged as an ad. This means that Instagram's algorithms will automatically push your posts up which increases their visibility in the news feed of every Instagram user.

The only disadvantage to this is that your content is immediately identified as an ad by users as well. This means that they can ignore it even more if they feel that whatever your publishing does not interest them.

A. Linking

By switching to a business profile, the No Linking limitation mentioned a few paragraphs before is immediately done away with. Now, as a business profile, you can add links to your content and your Stories which should drive traffic to whatever page you currently have in the Internet.

A Word of Advice

The Switch to Business Profile is only available at the very first instance that you set up your profile. Once you have chosen to have a private or business profile, you can't switch from either later on.

Once you feel confident with your choices, select Done and your profile is ready.

To Wrap Things Up....

The essence is that Instagram is a fairly easy platform to get yourself familiarized with. After setting up an account and getting to know the different content creation options being offered there, you should have your own official Instagram account for the business.

But this does leave a question: just exactly WHAT are you going to publish there. Yes, we know that it's going to be images. But what kind of images should you publish there that would resonate the most with your target audience?

Chapter 2: The Content Creation Process

It's an oft-repeated phrase in the world of online marketing that "Content is King". From the blogs that you read to the images that you share and post, content is always the primary way of getting your point across the Internet. This also means that most of your strategies online will deal with the creation and publishing of such content.

But what exactly is content and how do you create good ones? To answer those questions, there are a few things that you need to understand first.

Why Original Content Matters

There is this idea that content creation is a rather daunting task. After all, you would be creating something that may or may not be liked by everybody else in the market, and this affects the success of your brand in the Internet.

That pressure alone is enough to scare a lot of people from creating otherwise unique and engaging content. However, there are a few benefits as to why you'd rather deal with content creation anyway. Here are some of them:

1. Becoming Credible

Consumers nowadays are more fickle and discerning as ever. They are not so easy today to convince to be loyal to your brand as things were in the past. No amount of expensive marketing campaigns will ever be enough to compel a person to always part with their hard earned cash whenever they encounter your brand in the market.

Unless, however, if you can convince them to do such by earning their trust first. This, in turn, requires you to provide them with something valuable like information that they can use in practical situations through your content. The more value you provide and the more consistent you are with such, the easier it will be for people to trust you.

2. Response to Change

It is no secret that industries change especially in the online world. Changes in government regulations and even the climate can affect how people regard certain businesses and brands.

The best strategy that any content creator can use, then, is to push content that would tackle and address such changes to get their name across the market.

For example, the US Government might start imposing huge tariffs on other countries like China. Or what if a new law is passed that is life changing for many people, such as same sex marriage? What you could do in this regard is to start talking about that issue on your content and find a way to incorporate it into your marketing campaigns. Note, however, that it's best to be careful about this as well. It has to be relevant to your audience as much as possible.

If you can even talk and predict how such changes can affect the market, you are putting your brand at an advantageous position as "the business who called it" when such changes do take effect.

It takes a bit of inspiration from Journalism, in actuality. If you are the first to publish content that covers new changes in the market or the world, the more valuable your brand will be to the rest of the market.

3. The SEO Process

Content Creation and the Search Engine Optimization process have always gone hand in hand. In fact, the visibility of your content to your audiences will be determined by the search results pages by way of their algorithms.

Back then, list-type articles were all the rage as Google's previous algorithm deemed it so. However, when the Panda algorithm was implemented, the focus shifted to problem-solving information.

How search engines rank content is fairly straightforward. Whenever a query was put in, the search bots would scour the entire Internet to find key words and phrases that would match what was being asked. The more that bots find those words, the more visible that page or content will be in the results pages. Search engines do not reveal the specific algorithms but there are other factors as well including whether or not your content is deemed reliable or valuable.

This can be a double-edged sword on your part. If the kind of content that you produce does not meet the standard of search engine bots, you will find that its rankings will drop in the results pages within an instant. However, this is not the end to that content's usefulness which conveniently leads to the next point which is...

4. Potential for Re-purposing

The most seasoned of content creators know that there is more than one way to use content. Let us say that you have created an article about the best cleaning solutions for, say, wooden countertops. That's one way of conveying your message.

But there are other ways to do it. You can make an infographic out of your article and post it on Instagram. You can take still from a video and post it there while inviting others to visit your YouTube page.

There are even entire Podcasts made using only one article as a script while the rest of the people there add on to what has already been addressed in the primary content. The point is that the possibilities for saying the same thing over and over again without being redundant is endless if you are that creative.

5. Better Conversion Rates

The ultimate goal of content has always been to compel people to purchase a product or service that you might be offering. However, this can't be done if they (a) don't know you or (b) don't trust you at all.

Content that is made well can make your brand even more visible to end users which increases traffic to your site. The more value you provide for each content you make, the easier it is for a person to convert from an audience member to a paying and loyal customer to the business.

In essence, once a person thinks that you are trustworthy source of practical knowledge, they would hesitate less to consume what you have to offer. Even if they have to constantly part with their money just to get what you are promising to them.

The Pillars of Content Creation

So how does one go about creating content that is unique and effective for any sort of online campaign? The process can actually differ from one content type to another and from site to site but they cover the same aspects. In fact, every good content out there passes through five pillars.

1. Planning

After all, you can't create what you have never visualized. To plan content, you need to do several things:

a. **Identify the Target Market** - Naturally, you have to know who you are going to expose your marketing content to and this would include learning what topics, problems, and issues would resonate with these people the most.

b. **Your Goals -** What are you hoping to achieve from your marketing campaign? Do you want your brand's awareness to increase? Or do you want to expand and tap into new markets? Or perhaps your content is there to drive traffic and online sales for the business? Whatever your goals, you have to write them in paper.

c. **Know the Platform and Tools -** As was stated, the best kind of content are those that are native to platform. Take the time to familiarize yourself with the language and culture of Instagram and master every tool that the site gives to your disposal.

2. Creation/Production

This is where the bulk of the content creation process will be focused at. Once you have identified your target market and ideal marketing channel, you should now identify the kinds of topics that you want to talk about.

Whatever topic that you should choose, make it sure that it is highly relevant to the market or, at the very least, something that they are familiar with. This is also where things like keyword searches will become important for the SEO process.

You should also identify the purpose of your content. Does it inform or entertain? Does it want to inspire or convert people into customers? The goal you have for that content will affect its overall tone.

You should also consider where you are going to source your content with. Curating and crowdfunding are good alternatives if you are not that good in creating your own content. However, for the best results, it is best that you create your own content.

3. Optimization

Once content has been created, you should then make it a point to make it as highly engaging and consumable as possible. The first check it has to pass is on Factuality. Everything contained there must be true and accurate as readers might also be verifying what you are saying from outside sources. Errors in fact might even affect your brand's reputation especially if you do it more than once.

The next check is on Grammar and Structure. Does it follow a strong and clear narrative from start to finish? Does everything inside that content work in proving (or disproving) a certain issue?

Does every paragraph follow basic subject-verb agreements? Can anyone go through what you just made without getting lost in between the beginning and the end? These are just some of the things that you have to check to prevent issues later on.

This is also why it is better that you would invest on an expert editor to check on the quality of your content as they are the counterpart of creators. You may even do it yourself provided that you have the time and skills to do so. Either way, you have to make sure that whatever you publish has gone through stringent checks in quality.

4. Marketing

Aside from creating content, you should also build interest for it. Think of it as something similar to what videogame developers and publishers do every June with the E3 Show. There, they would release trailers and demos for their upcoming products to generate buzz prior to their respective releases.

For content, there are multiple ways to do this. The most common method is through social media where you post updates regarding upcoming content. Everyone that has been linked to your profile will see the update and would theoretically be interested in whatever will come out.

Another method is through e-mail where you send an email to all those subscribed to your mailing list to notify them that something is about to be released.

Either strategy is way more effective than traditional marketing as you are already targeting people who already have an experience with your brand or are exposed to it on a regular basis. This means that they would show less hesitation in consuming whatever you are trying to offer to them.

5. Publishing and Measuring Results

Once enough hype has been built for your business, all that is left to do is to publish it. However, this is not the end of the process.

Once you have published your content, the next thing to do is to measure how it is being engaged in the market. What many content creators forget to do is to constantly interact with their target audience.

Due to the level of interaction provided on the Internet, they may want you to clarify on an issue you raised in your content or correct you with certain facts if they think that what you were presenting was not truly accurate.

Either way, this provides an opportunity to interact with your audience which further drives traffic to your pages and makes your content even more relevant.

After a few days or weeks, you must then take note of the actual level of engagement generated by your content from the likes, shares, and even comments. You should take note of any issue that your audience pointed out regarding your work and the subtopics that they were engaged with the most. This will give you an idea as to what to publish next and help you improve your skills as a creator.

What Makes Great Content?

Content may come in all shapes and sizes in marketing. However, what can make content be considered as good? There is no definitive answer to that but the best ones always seemingly follow a scheme.

Content Classification

To make this easier, what you will have to remember is that content can come in three major categories which are:

A. Product - this is basically the types of content that offer something tangible to your audiences be it products or services.

B. Role - Content of this type assumes a role of sorts in relation to the life of every audience member. What is that content trying to do for the audience? What goal is it trying to achieve for them? What are the questions that it is trying to answer? Identifying the role that the ad will take will determine the narrative that it is going to tell to its audience.

C. Emotion - A content of this classification is designed to connect with audiences at a personal, intimate, and emotional level. The point of this content type's existence is to evoke some sort of emotional response in its viewers. Or, at least, it does provide them with another perspective on how things should be viewed at.

So, which then of these three types is the content that you should be publishing in Instagram?

The answer is all of them. Each type has its own strengths and weaknesses which means that a diverse portfolio of marketing content that focuses on one or another is going to help you in the long run.

The point is that you don't favor one over the other. Focusing too much on pushing your product or services prevents you from making a personal connection with your audiences, thereby ruining the opportunity to make them convert. On the other hand, if you focus too much on triggering emotions, you run the risk of confusing your audience as to exactly what you want for them to do.

Thinking Like a Journalist

The best kind of content out there, if you think about, serves a purpose. If a person goes to your Instagram page, they are most likely not there just to ogle at your pictures. They might be there to seek information, confirm their biases, be entertained, or get the persuasion that they need to complete the sales process.

Whatever the reason, the point is that you should put out content that should be able to convince your audience that you have something worthwhile to offer. Remember that making people convert is hard these days without you offering something tangible to them first.

And there is no other profession out there that can convince people to think and act differently than a Journalist. So why not copy their style for your marketing content? Here's how:

1. Identify Your Angle

Journalists always write their story from an angle or a perspective of sorts. Think of it this way: there is always more than one way to view things which means that no two people viewing the same thing can ever share the same exact point of view. As such, the best journalists create their content using an angle that their readers can relate to.

For instance, if you are a cleaning product supplier, you may produce content that shows how your products are being used for practical purposes. The angle of the narrative that your content conveys will actually serve as a point of entry to your audience towards the customer conversion process. This is because you are giving them an idea as to how to process the information that you are about to give to them.

2. Start Right

The impression that your introductory lines will affect the overall reception of your content. If the angle defines the narrative, then the introduction will start the process of turning your ideas into actionable responses.

More often than not, it is in the introduction where you will spend a lot of time of as this will dictate the mood of your overall story. To make it easier on your part, make the introduction answer the 5 Ws:

- Who

- What

- When

- Why

- Where

This should start your story within just the first sentence if done right.

3. Give Your Content Humanity

Emotions play a vital role to the reception of your content which is why you should give your content a "human" factor. For instance, a quote from a popular person gives credence to any point or argument that you might raise.

On a more direct note, you can always use user-generated content like testimonials and reviews to get the point of your Instagram content across. And speaking of getting to the point...

4. Do Not Waste Words

Given the image-heavy format of Instagram, it is best that you directly convey your message to your target audience. Introduce the problem, offer the solution, and then make a call to action.

Never, in any case, go off into long tangents or digress from the point. You should keep your audience's interest for the story at a high so they won't scroll down to the next content on their food. Say what needs to be said but do not leave out any important detail.

The Call to Action

As was mentioned, it is your content that would do all the convincing your audience that your offer is great. However, it is at the CTA where the final push towards conversion occurs.

So what does a good Call to Action look like? Here are a few qualities that you should include in yours.

1. Value

Always remember that people rarely buy these days just for the sake of it. If you want them to do something for you, make sure that you offer something of equal value in return. As such, the CTA should summarize the main points of your content to give your viewers the idea that what they are about to do is ultimately beneficial for them.

2. Visibility

Your CTA should be placed somewhere in the content where it is easily seen and distinguished. You can do this by putting them on a separate paragraph if your content is text-based or as a caption for images. The goal is to get the viewer's attention long enough to decide whether or not they want to complete the sales process.

3. Personality

One quality that the normal, everyday person has that no company could ever compete with is the ability to be trusted more. CTAs that offer an intimate and unique twist can connect with people more than those that are just blatant with their marketing. After all, there is a huge difference between saying "buy our stuff!" with "come and have a wonderful experience with us!".

4. Clarity

Being clear is always recommended as the overall goal of marketing is to compel people to do something. Your CTA must let the viewers know EXACTLY what you want from them and what it is they will be signing up for. Also, you have to highlight and summarize all the properties that make your offering stand out from the competition.

5. Shortness

CTAs don't have the luxury of a space big enough for you explain everything to the viewers. Instead, they only say a few words that convey what has already been established in your primary content.

And if you think one paragraph is too short for that, remember that you can now link your content to your webpages since your profile is a Business type. Your viewers can complete the conversion process to wherever your links take them to.

The Caption

In Instagram, the picture might be the one doing all the selling but it is the caption that eases in your audiences for what is to come. That is why you need to make it as catchy as possible.

As such, here are a few tips to remember when creating your title.

1. Be Emotional

Do you know who appreciates adjectives like "state of the art", "cutting edge", and "top of the line"? Robots.

If you want to get your audience's attention, look for words that would definitely trigger an emotional response. Instead of "Best", why not use "essential"? After all, consumers are looking for something that they need, not a symbol of perfection. If you can make that human connection, you should have your viewer's attention hooked right from the start.

2. Tap into Logic

Again, a bit of word play will help you in getting your reader's attention. Once you have made that emotional connection, you can start on appealing to the rational part of the brain. So words like "act", "do", "think", and "reason" will be effective in this next part.

Also, you should adopt a more authoritative tone at this part of your headline. Words like "Facts" and "secrets" give off an air of credibility which gives a subliminal clue for the brain to pay attention to whatever you are going to say next.

If possible, never use vague or generic words like "thing". Most readers would find that rather mundane which ruins their engagement to the content to follow.

3. Be Bold

Your caption should offer something interesting to readers without giving away too much of the message. Will the image or link teach them something new? Will they get a new piece of information that will finally answer the most pressing questions of their life? Will it tell them about where to get the best Thin-Crust Pizzas in (insert city here)?

Whatever the case, make sure that the caption actually challenges your viewers to go through the content and to links being provided. Once you have their attention, all that is left to do is to hope that whatever your image is saying will actually live up to the promise set in the caption.

To Conclude

There is a certain art to content creation, undoubtedly. You can't just approach this aspect of advertising with a purely mechanical disposition. Being knowledgeable about certain topics is good but you have to also be passionate with them. Passion is the one final element that will ultimately push your content to convert people into customers loyal to the brand.

Do it right and you will not only produce content that is well created and highly engaging but ones that consistently make a connection with whatever target audience you have in mind.

Chapter 3: The Power of Images

Can a Picture really say a thousand words?

The short answer is yes.

In fact, the success of social media sites like Facebook and Instagram are proof that image-based content maintains a strong presence in the online world nowadays.

But why should you even consider using them aside from the fact that they are the primary commodity in Instagram? The reason for this is that it has always been a rather potent medium when it comes to conveying marketing messages.

Why Do Consumers Prefer Visuals?

Compared to text-based and sound-based interactions, image-based content tends to be more preferred by the average online audience member. The primary reason for this is that imagery as a communication tool is easier to process and is more visually arresting.

Of course, this means that visuals can spike online engagement to a considerable degree. In fact, in a report by Buffer, it has been found out that in the twitter platform, content with images tend to receive 18% more click-throughs and 89% more favorites compared to those with no images at all.

In addition, content with images to enjoy as much as 150% more shares and comments compared to other forms of content save for videos. And not only are consumers engaging with visuals more, they tend to remember the messages better with the aid of visuals.

An infographic shared by Adweek shows that 80% people remember marketing messages more versus the 20% who do so through text. In short, images make a more lasting impression on its own compared to any other available format out there.

All in all, visual content can be used effectively for various marketing content. If done right, they might pose a number of advantages which include:

- Easy customer retention

- Immediate impact in customers

- Ease of presentation and processing of information

- Faster mental stimulation

- Grabs customer attention better

- Help customers in making a purchasing decision

The Anatomy of a Good Instagram Post

So, if visuals are a fairly effective marketing medium, how should you include it as part of your Instagram campaign? A good Instagram post, regardless of purpose, always contains several qualities which are as follows:

1. Visual Quality

This is the most basic concept that you need to master in Instagram. People only flock to your account if you provide them with high-quality visual content.

Of course, high quality visuals can be made possible by investing in state of the art equipment. But there is more to visual quality than using the most modern DLSR camera model.

The skills of the photographer itself will also matter in taking that perfect shot. This will be discussed later on.

2. A Compelling Caption

As was mentioned a chapter ago, your caption can draw in people to your image. As such, you need something that should be compelling.

The tone of the caption must match with the message you are trying to convey. If you are not sure with what you want to do with your caption, then at the very least make it inviting.

However, the caption must always include a link that directs people to whatever webpage you have, preferably the main page or the sales page. This is also where a good CTA will be included as it will direct people to do something to get something in return.

3. The Hashtag

They may look like unnecessary additions to your image but hashtags actually make them more visible and engaging to the community. How this works is quite simple: when people search for something like #fashion on Instagram, the site's algorithms will scour the entire site for content that contains that hashtag.

In essence, it is like a miniature version of Search Engine Optimization. The more relevant your hashtags are, the quicker it will be for people to find your content amidst the veritable sea of images on the platform.

4. Engaging with the Community

This is not exactly an inherent feature of Instagram posts but a direct result of good ones. Instagrammers who know the trends of the platform know it is essential to constantly engage with their audience.

How this is done is actually quite simple. When you post something, people are typically going to comment especially if they are interested with the topic. You can engage with your community by replying to these comments which, in turn, generates more replies.

In essence, setting up a conversation with your customers is a good way of establishing rapport with your audience. And, of course, the more people find you trustworthy, the easier it is for them to convert into paying customers.

5. Sizing, Specs, and Dimensions

Instagram may automatically resize large images but the people behind the platform would rather that you follow certain specifications when uploading images to the site.

For images, the dimensions should follow the basic shape of the square. The reason for this is that the shape allows it to easily readjust for different screen sizes and orientations.

For videos, they should be no more than 15 seconds, the wordings must be at 20 words per frame, and is optimized for sound-off viewing. If you follow these rules, you should be able to create Instagram posts that would be interesting at the very least and highly engaged with at the most.

The Types of Visual Content that Would (Most Likely) Go Viral

What kind of visual content should you use for your Instagram campaigns? What you will use depends greatly on what purpose you want to achieve.

When it comes to online campaigns, there are several visual contents that you can use which are:

1. Infographics

The perfect marriage between visual and text-based content, Infographics are best described as articles in image form as they contain a lot of information presented in a highly visual manner. It is a far less intimidating option as to purely text articles and the information is easier to process and understand.

The only problem with this, however, is that they are rarely compatible in Instagram due to their size. At best, you can only link to such infographics which will take your viewers to a separate page.

Also, they are quite dependent on statistical data. Unless you have a lot of those on hand, there is no point to create one yourself.

2. Photos

Conventional photos are important for several reasons. For businesses, they allow viewers to make a personal connection with the brand as they are quite eye-catching and relatable. Also, this gives businesses the chance to let people take a peek behind the scenes and learn more of the people running the business.

Also, photos are great for showcasing your products and services. In fact, you can display your entire product catalogue in Instagram and link it to your main website. This takes off a huge data load from your site (which makes it load faster) while still increasing traffic in between it and your Instagram profile.

3. Videos

If infographics mix text and images, then videos mix text, images, sound, and motion. It is the perfect blend of every known content format out there and it can help you convey your message at a far easier and faster rate.

The only disadvantage with videos is the demanding production value behind them. It takes quite a lot of effort to capture videos, edit them, and then publish them on the page. Also, remember that Instagram allows only for no more than a minute of video footage so you need to make a video that says what you need to say within that time frame.

But videos do have other benefits offered which include:

- Improved customer retention

- Better SEO ranking

- Higher rate of engagement in customers and audience members; and

- A stronger personal connection between businesses and their customers.

4. The Inspirational Quote

For pure emotional appeal, there is no other visual format out there that can beat inspirational quotes. Why they are highly engaged with is quite simple. Everybody needs that pep talk, regardless of where they get it.

Also, there is no strong motivator towards completing the sales conversion process than, well, being Motivated. If you can get people the emotional fix that they need, they are more susceptible towards any marketing message that you might want to convey.

One neat advantage of inspirational images is that they are quite easy to create. You only need that quote and find an appropriate image such as a relaxing view of the sunset or, better yet, the picture of the person who said it.

5. Screenshots

Content of this type is usually made when you want to highlight a specific part that would otherwise not be noticed by everybody else. For instance, there might be this memorable (or, in recent times, meme-able) moment in your video.

You can immediately create a screen shot through the Print Screen option on your keyboard, the screenshot feature on your mobile phone, or any third party image capturing device.

As such, screenshots can be used for a number of content including instructionals, commentaries, and even product reviews and testimonials.

6. Quizzes and Other Gamified Content

One great way to drive up engagement for your content is to ask a question. After all, nothing can illicit responses more than something that is quizzical by design.

Also, quizzes can give this impression that your brand is hip, smart, and creative. Creating quizzes is also fairly easy and straightforward. One variant of gamified content you could use is also trivia as it turns information regarding your product or service into something interesting or, better yet, useful.

Puzzles are also a great image content for you to use as it taps into the more logical part of the human brain. By encouraging them to answer the puzzle, you increase the click-through rates for your content to a considerable degree.

7. Memes

A fairly new trend, memes are a great way to increase your brand's engagement with younger demographics. It also helps that memes are mostly visual based content and, for most of the time, illicit laughs.

Memes like Grumpy Cat and the Condescending Willy Wonka are examples of memes that advertisers have used for their visual marketing. If you do insist on using memes, it is best that you understand the joke behind the image. There have been far too many times when marketers used memes incorrectly, resulting in a tone-deaf or way-too-trying-hard marketing message.

How to Capture an Instagram-Worthy Picture

As was stated, there are some benefits to be had from creating your own visual content. Marketing photos are perhaps the easiest to create as you already have one when you push that button on your camera.

But, of course, only good photos have the highest rate of engagement in the platform. To truly capture moments that are worthy of being "Instagrammed", there are a few principles that you have to master first.

1. Lighting

This is the foundation of all good photos as even the best-looking subjects out there won't evoke any response from your audience if they can't see it. If possible, only use natural light as they create photos that are brighter and richer in color.

Flash photos, on the other hand, might be bright but the glare of the flash might obscure some important details in your picture. This results in a bright but washed out picture.

If shooting outdoors is not an option, you must take photos near windows or in a well-lit room.

If you have to take the photo at evening, find a good source of ambient light like a street lamp or a nearby store window.

2. Exposure

Sure, you can always brighten up a photo with some good editing tools. However, an image that was overexposed to begin with is not worth saving.

Phone cameras have an advantage over professional cameras as you can adjust the exposure by tapping the screen up or down before taking the picture.

The rule of thumb in exposure is that the subject itself must be clearly visible but its contours and details must not fade out from the image.

3. Timing

There is this term among photographers called the "Golden Hour". this is the time when the sun is at its lowest point in the horizon, resulting in truly breathtaking pictures.

As such, you need to find the right time to capture your images. If you can, always take your picture during cloudy days. They diffuse a lot of the sun's light which results in a softer effect.

4. Composition

This refers to the arrangement of the photos which includes the shapes, textures, colors, and other elements that make up your image.

When balancing the composition of your image, always follow the Rule of Thirds. Divide your image into a 3x3 grid and align the subjects in a photo along the lines to create a balance. In this instance, your subject must be at the centermost box to balance the image.

Alternatively, you can employ what is called as balanced asymmetry where the subject is off-center. However, this should be balanced by another element to fill in the void left by the shift in alignments. For example, your subject of a flower might be placed to the left or the right but this should be counterbalanced by the sky or a near wall opposite to where it stands.

You can do the rule of Thirds by turning on the gridline option on your camera's setting. This should help you line up the elements better for taking the shot.

5. Angle

The most common thing that people do when taking a picture is hold the camera at eye level and click away. The end result is decent but nowhere near dynamic or interesting.

Try some weird angles to give your image new perspectives. You may view the subject from the bottom or you can climb up to something and take your pictures from above.

Some photographers would even lie on their stomachs or balance themselves between rocks just to take that perfectly angled shot. It's not necessary for you to make yourself uncomfortable to try new angles. Just don't settle for the usual angle if you want your images to look like they are in motion.

6. Framing

Instead of zooming in, you should leave space around the subject that you are focusing on. This allows outside elements to add more visual oomph to your image.

For instance, a picture of a glass at night is already great but you can make it even more interesting by giving space for the night sky above. This adds an air of "mystery" or "melancholy" to your image which makes it more memorable to the viewer.

For camera phones, you have to tap into the focal subject to make the camera focus on it. This is because they have an automatic zoom function which shrinks the field of view. This means that your image is already pre-cropped which limits your options for editing later on.

7. Leading

Leading lines are invisible marks on your image that draw the eye of the viewer and gives more depth or motion. Even natural elements like roads, waves, and buildings can make your image deeper than it really is, resulting in a semi-3D Effect.

8. Depth

The elements outside of the subject can also bring in a layer of depth to your image. As such, do not ever zoom in to your images before taking the picture.

There is no telling what other interesting things outside of your image's subject that could make things even more interesting to the final image. That tree in the distance or people on the background can add another layer to the image and prevents it from becoming flat.

This works well if there is a contrast between the subject and fore and backgrounds. For instance, if the object is motion, everything around it must stand still. Or if everything is in motion, the subject must lay still.

This clash of movement between the subject and the elements surrounding it will make your image stand out even more when you publish it on Instagram.

To Conclude

Making or capturing images for your Instagram marketing efforts might take some getting used to. After all, nobody became an expert photographer or graphic artist overnight.

However, practice is the key to making it right with your visual content. If done right, you should be able to make some interesting photos which will draw in a lot of viewers to your account.

Chapter 4: Understanding Your Instagram Audience

The end goal of your Instagram marketing is always Visibility. But who should you be visible to? The site is home to more than 1 billion active users per month and surely there should be a fraction of that population who is going to take you up on your offer.

Fortunately, every kind of person and business has an audience in any social media platform they use. It is up to them to find out who these people are and what to do to get a hold of them.

What Are Analytics?

By the end of this decade, Instagram is not only becoming an important marketing tool but also a viable place to build a community in. In short, everyone who wants to survive in the world of Social Media should consider venturing into Instagram before it gets too big.

But this does pose a question: How could anyone tell that Instagram is the best place for them to be? Or, to be more technical about it, how would you know that your marketing strategies are working there?

The answer is Analytics.

In Instagram, there are analytics being provided that help you understand how each of your posts are performing and the overall trend for your account. This is a bit different from metrics as analytics show your account's marketing potential as a whole. Metrics, on the other hand, show

To make this simpler to understand, here's a distinction. The number of followers you have is considered a Metric. The rate of how your follower base in the platform is growing at a certain period of time is an Analytic rate.

But let's not get ahead of ourselves. Here are the 5 Metrics that you should be aware of in order to do Analytics right.

Follower Growth

This may be the simplest metric but it is undoubtedly one of the most important ones. The number of people who follow you on the site will affect the overall performance of your marketing there in a number of ways.

Think of it this way: In order to target people on the platform, you need to have Reach. Through the people that follow you, your brand gets exactly that. The more people engage with your account, the more clicks you will get. And the stronger your traffic is in between your channels, the more visible your brand will be online.

Follower Count vs. Follower Growth: What's the Difference?

But, as was stated, having a large number of followers is no longer enough. You also need to track how quickly your follower base is growing over time.

For instance, if your follower base increased by 1% on March, another 2% on April, and another 1% on May, it is a telltale sign that your brand's reach is steadily yet constantly expanding.

On the flip side, if it grows by 8% on May, then 2% on June, and then 1% on July, it might imply that your base is not as growing steadily as you would like. Perhaps there is something in your strategy that is no longer working.

Worse is when your follower base grows by the negatives every month. This is a telltale sign that you are losing subscribers to your account.

Sadly, the growth rate of your Follower base is not something that is readily provided in Instagram's Insights feature. To get this you have the option of counting your followers each month on a spreadsheet and calculate the change in percentage yourself or have a separate Instagram analytics program do the recording and analysis for you.

Demographics

Aside from knowing the size of your follower base, you'd also have to know its composition: just *who* are your followers? Regardless of what you have set as a goal for your marketing campaign, a crucial understand on the profile of your follower/potential customer will help you hone your content to match what they need or expect from you.

For instance, you might think that your brand is catering towards young American teens but find out that most of your Instagram follower base are middle-aged adults in Europe.

This was the same predicament that befell on Mattel in the mid-2000s when they were marketing their show My Little Pony towards kids only to find out that a larger portion of their fanbase belongs to the Adult demographic;

and are males for a reason. Thankfully, they managed to find a balance between the two groups and the MLP brand remains strong even up to 2019.

The point is that knowing what composes your audience demographics, whether or not they fit the persona of what you think is your primary audience, can tip you off on how to better mold your marketing messages. You might even discover new niches in the market that your brand has yet to tap or, to that effect, nobody else has.

Fortunately, the Insights feature can give you good analytics of the composition of your audience. You can even tell which gender your brand caters to the most and from what regions across the world.

How to Make the Most of Your Audience Demographics

Before anything else, you need to have a customer persona set up for your marketing. These are a list of qualities that your ideal customers would display which helps you create your marketing content. A guide on identifying your personas can be found in the following section.

You must use this persona, then, as a benchmark to check if what you think your audiences are would match the profile of the people that do actually compose your audience in real time.

Is there any difference between your personas and your actual audience? What similarities do they share? In what way can you tap these new niches without alienating your primary audience?

Alternatively, if you think that your marketing is a bid too broad, you can use the Analytics to identify the actual profile of most of your customers. This will help you laser-focus your efforts into targeting these specific individuals in the market.

Website Clicks

Here is one bitter pill that anyone on Social Media should swallow: Followers and Fans are not automatically Customers. Just because someone has shown interest for the brand, it does not mean that there is a potential for income there.

This is what happened to the Star Wars brand who saw a dip in box office returns for their last two films despite seemingly strong followings in

Social Media. On a lesser scale, this is what happened to a young Instagrammer named Arianne Renee who failed to sell 36 T-Shirts of her own making despite having 2 million followers on the site.

What you should be looking for is the number of times that people were so convinced by your marketing that they actually visited your other channels or, to that effect, your main web page. This is where click through rates come into play and they happen to tell you accurately whether or not your Instagram marketing is driving up traffic to your pages.

For instance, if your marketing campaign contains a link to your main webpage and people click it, they would be taken to that page. This counts as one click-through and is a strong indicator that your web traffic is not stagnating.

This metric is quite crucial if your marketing campaign's overall goal is to drive traffic to your webpages. Alternatively, it might be not as important if your overall goal is brand awareness.

Of course, a lot of click-throughs means that your website is hosting a lot of visitors every day. That won't give you the assurance that each visitor is converting into a customer but it does tell that your campaign has the potential to eventually compel people to do so.

Also, if your site's traffic is unchanged, then perhaps you should consider changing the tone of your CTA. Perhaps it is not too forceful or effective in making people visit your other channels.

How to Track Web Traffic at Instagram

Fortunately, the Insights section can help you get an idea as to your page's outgoing traffic. It is at the Activity Section under the Interactions tab. This should tell you how many people clicked to your bio over the past few days or weeks.

This is a good start for measuring your traffic but it's not the only method. You can also use Google's Analytics program or add a UTM Code to the link in your Bio. The latter will tell you how many of those click-throughs actually led to a sales conversion.

Lastly, you can use Facebook's Pixels feature. It is also effective in tracking outgoing traffic from your Social Media pages and tallying up all conversions that were not only started but actually finished.

Reach

Although this is not a key indicator of performance for online marketing campaigns, it does tell you how much of a buzz your brand is generating in the market. Reach is the metric that measures how many people have seen your posts. This includes the people who saw your picture/video/any other content and those that watched your Story.

You might be thinking, *Isn't this like Impressions, though?* Not really.

Impressions is counted every time your content is seen. Reach, on the other hand, is counted, every time a unique user does something with your content. As such, it is better to look at the Reach than the Impressions that your content makes.

In fact, Impressions is more like a vanity metric as it doesn't tell you how many times that person ignored your content before actually interacting with it. Reach will tell you that and also how many people have seen your content, leading to a more accurate measurement.

Why Reach Really Matters

In essence, Reach is important as it tells you one of the most important things in Instagram for marketers: whether or not your posts are showing up in the feeds of the people that you are targeting. There are a lot of factors that could affect reach such as the level of engagement for your account, the time people spend perusing your content, and even the time when you published it.

As such, reach can tell you in general terms how popular your content is as well as if it has good timing and an interesting hook for engagement. For example, a high percentage of reach could tell you that a lot of people are spending time looking at your photos as opposed to merely glancing at them from the feed.

Alternatively, it could mean that your content schedule is working for you as people are engaging at it immediately after publishing it. Or perhaps it is a bit of both which tells you that your marketing is effective even if only at a technical standpoint.

But what if your reach is getting lower? You could consider reorganizing the timing of your content. Or you could look at the next most important metric which is...

Engagement

If Content is the King on the Internet, then Engagement is Instagram's very own feudal lord. To put it less creatively, engagement is the most crucial metric that you could ever refer to when it comes to your marketing campaigns on the site.

Engagement can tell you how much of a connection you are making with your followers and potential customers as well as other influential people and brands. In fact, when it comes to Engagement, Instagram has the highest levels of such compared to other social media sites.

Why is Engagement really important on Instagram? The reason is that the algorithms bump up those posts that get a lot of engagement. In essence, the more engagement each posts you have gets, the more visible it will be on the site.

For Instagram, engagement comes in the form of the number of likes, comments, and shares that your posts get. And you can see this by adjusting the settings of your Content tab found at the Insights panel.

What is Engagement Rate?

Although engagement is a good metric, there is an even better metric in the form of engagement rate. It tells you the percentage of the people that actually engaged with your content and compare it to the reach that it enjoyed from.

For instance, one post might have a high reach but a low engagement rate. This means a lot of people saw it but not a lot interacted with it.

Alternatively, if a post has a low reach but a high enough engagement level, it could tell you that whatever message that post contained reached the right people and caused them to respond.

So what is a good engagement rate? There is no hard and fast rule for that but experts do encourage that they reach at least 1.75% as of the most recent months. So, if a post has 5000 in reach, then it should strive to at least get 87.5 in engagements.

The Ultimate Takeaway: When all is said and done, these metrics will tell you how much your content is being treated at in Instagram's market. That is something that you absolutely have no control over in the same way that you have no control over how people perceive your brand in the real world.

What it does great, however, is giving you clues and hints as to how to better approach your market. The metrics can help you predict how people are going to react when exposed to the same message or a variant of it. This way, you can carefully improve on your message until you reach that point when you can target your audiences confidently in the platform.

Finding (And Reaching) Your Target Audience

Now that you know how people behave statistics-wise on Instagram, the next part will involve finding the people who will most likely consume what you have to offer. Remember that you don't have to target every Instagrammer out there for your campaigns, just the right ones.

With that in mind, there are few things that you have to remember when finding your audience and then reaching out the them. They are as follows:

1. Define Your Audience

You may ask "what's the point of even having an idea as to who my target audience is?" After all, whoever they are, they will come to your profile if they like what you offer, right?

You would actually have to do this for two reasons:

a. It will Challenge Your Assumptions - There is a great chance that the actual target audience for your brand is bigger and more diverse than what you thought of. You might even discover new niches in the market that your brand has not put in the effort of targeting in the post.

But, of course, with knowledge comes the need to adjust. Now that you know that there are more people out there that have an interest for your brand, would like you to adjust your marketing efforts to also include their needs and expectations.

Going back to the My Little Pony problem, did Mattel choose to ignore that older demographic? No. That is because these individuals had a stronger purchasing agency and can even influence their children to consume Mattel's products.

So what they did is change their marketing to include these people and even made some tweaks on their product to make them more appealing to the new demographic.

In Instagram, you will discover a lot of new niches that might show an interest for your brand. By identifying these people, you can come up with strategies that better target them which increases engagement for your brand.

b. It Will Make Things Easier for You - For marketers, there is nothing more frustrating than the Unknown. This is for the reason that the unknown is hard to predict and even harder to adapt to.

By identifying the various profiles of your potential customers, you have a more solid foundation to stand on when it comes to promoting your brand at Instagram. In essence, you are giving Method to the Madness that is online marketing.

2. Identify Your Personas

First of all, what is a Persona? It is basically a set of qualities and characteristics shared by your assumed consumers that will tell you how they are going to react to your marketing.

It's a bit different from Demographics as your Personas are based on your assumptions while Demographics are based on cold, hard, statistical facts. They may share some similarities but rarely do you get a demographic that perfectly fits your marketing personas.

Setting up one is fairly easy. All you have to do is to come up with a list of behaviors that people display when exposed to your brand in other channels. Perhaps your Facebook community liked that one marketing campaign of yours. You could use that data to form a sequence of response of sorts to every marketing strategy that you have used.

Next, you will then give them a face by categorizing all these qualities into different sets of "identities". These identities can then be based on basic classifiers like age, sex, social status, income level, and region. Perhaps people in Age Group A would react differently compared to Age Group B. Or perhaps Income Level A would be more recipient to your marketing than Income Level B.

Doing so gives you some rudimentary customer personas that you could refer to when creating your marketing strategies. Of course, you could use these personas as a benchmark when identifying your actual audience in Instagram.

3. Reach Out

Once you have segmented your target audiences and know what they care about, it is time to start reaching out to those audiences. Just remember that each persona will require a different approach. However, just keep in mind a few things when trying to reach out to your different potential segments.

Mind the Timing

Using your Instagram's analytics, you should find out in what time of the day (your time zone, of course) when people interact with your content the most. The norm is that activity peaks just in between 5pm to 9pm, where people get off their work or school.

However, that is not exactly applicable in all instances as some demographics are active on other parts of the day or exclusively on a few days of the week. Whatever the case, Instagram's analytics tool will tell you when and where people interact with your content the most.

Find the Right Content

You should also identify what type of Instagram content people have engaged with your brand the most and what campaigns have worked well in the past few months, if any. This will tell you how the most on how to approach your target audience the best.

But a word of warning: just because something worked in the past, that does not mean it should work now. For instance, using a Meme might generate a lot of engagement in your past campaign but using the same meme for this new campaign might be detrimental. It's like telling a joke: it is only funny if you do it once.

Also, there might be some tweaks in Instagram's algorithms which causes the in-site search bots to push certain types of content more today than others in the past. As such, it is highly important that you do your research on current trends on social media and even Instagram's own policy changes. This way, changes won't surprise you and severely hurt your campaign's chance of success.

Study the Competition

Perhaps the most cost effective way of doing your research is just to observe what everybody else is doing. What are other brands similar to yours doing in Instagram? Are they succeeding there or do you think you can add a more effective twist to their strategies?

Whatever the case, the content published by your competitors can serve as a major source of inspiration; from a certain point of view. Perhaps one of their campaigns worked so well and it wouldn't hurt to do the same for your brand.

But, of course, there is a fine line between inspiration and downright being a copycat. Just take inspiration from what worked with your competitors but don't copy things point by point.

Leverage Instagram Stories

There are more than 500 thousand people around the world that use Instagram's Stories feature on a daily basis. There are quite a lot of features on offer which allow you to interact better with your audiences and enjoy from a more direct from of engagement with them.

Much of what you can do with the Stories feature will be discussed in detail on a later chapter but the point is that you should take advantage of this feature as much as you can. Find content that you can use to post there and keep track of your level of engagement there.

Use Hashtags Properly

Use the Follow feature to keep track of what niches in your target market care about the most in recent times. Of course, this means that the proper use of hashtags will make you more visible to Instagram as users and search bots can see your content quickly and consume the ones that they care about the most.

Of course, this is dependent on the fact that you have already identified your niche in the market. The more niches you can tap into, the more potential buyers you can attract to your brand.

4. Application

With these information, you can set up a rudimentary targeting scheme which may look like as follows:

Business Type: Finance

Product: Savings Program

Demographic: Males

Sub-Class: Late Teens to Adult, College-Level

Target With: Instagram Stories Re: Saving for the Future

Best Times to Post: 6-9PM

Competitors: Other Banks and Financial Institutions

Here's another example

Business Type: Bar

Product: Food and Drinks

Demographics; Adults, Working Class

Target With: Visual Campaigns that highlight bar's customer experience, food, and signature drinks.

Best Times to Post: 3-10PM

Competitors: Other bars and restaurants

Just remember, however, that just because one strategy hasn't been used in your industry or niche in the market that has not been tapped, that you should use them. For example, Adidas might have published an excellent Instagram campaign that extended their reach in the platform while also yielding in tons of engagement. It might even be featured by the media and hailed as one of the best Instagram campaigns of (insert year here).

Of course, you might be tempted to use that strategy for your brand. But here's the problem: Adidas is a clothing brand but you are not. Perhaps you are in banking in finance or perhaps you run a small bar. Using the same strategy might yield different results for your case, results that you may or may not like.

But this goes the other way, too. Just because you are not selling exactly the same products as other successful brands does not mean that you can't use the same tactics that they have employed. All that is needed here is a bit of common sense on your part. If you think it's going to work for your brand or not, take the time to do your research and run up some predictions here and there.

It pays to be extra careful with your campaigns right now given social media's current climate (which shall be tackled later on).

Using Influencers

In some cases, a lot of brands (especially the old-fashioned, brick and mortar types) are a "hard sell" in the online world. The reason for this is that things that made them relevant way back when the Internet was not a thing is no longer working these days.

You can't just tell people that your offerings are great and expect them to eat it all up. More often than not, the high degree of agency and access to information provided by the Internet will make these people highly doubtful of all that hyperbole that you've just told them.

The point is that conventional marketing strategies are not going to work on the newer demographics today, which are made up of the ones that we call "Millennials". But that does not mean that they won't listen to these marketing messages. It's just that they typically only do so if delivered by certain messengers. And this is where Influencers come into play.

It goes without saying that collaborating with an influencer can make for a sound marketing strategy regardless of what platform you choose to operate in. And luckily for you, Instagram is the home to many effective influencers like the Kardashians, Beyoncé, Dwayne "The Rock" Johnson, and Jay Alvarrez.

As such, here are a few things to remember when using Influencers to optimize their effects.

A. Match the Niche

Just because influencers have something called "clout", that does not mean that they have mass market appeal. Rather than finding the most popular people on Instagram to help your brand expand its reach, the more prudent tactic is to find the influencer that resonates most with your target market.

Make a list of speakers, industry authorities, celebrities, thought leaders, and other people that your target demographics are following on the platform. You can do this by doing a simple search on Google and determine which topics brands like yours tend to deal with. Then, make a list of names of the people that have tackled the same issues as these will be the most suitable influencers for your campaigns.

B. Assess, Assess, Assess

Once you have a list of potential influencers to tap, you must then determine how effective they are in regards to your brand. You can do this by looking at three factors which are:

- **Relevance** - Does everybody in the industry know who that influencer is? Does their style match the type of strategies that you usually employ?

You can determine this by taking a look at the type of content that they usually produce as their manner of speaking and style will tell you who they tend to reach out the most. After all, why use an influencer like the Paul Brothers or the Kardashians if you are not a) a fashion brand or b) marketing to teens?

- **Resonance** - Some influencers tend to create content that does not elicit the proper response with their audience. This is what is called being "tone deaf" and it can hurt your brand if they do this frequently.

Whenever an influencer does this, do they get a lot of dislikes compared to their likes? How about the number of shares and the quality of comments that such content generates? Also, you have to be careful as to how that influencer pushes their opinions around or weigh in on discussions especially in topics that you usually tackle.

- **Reach** - Take a look at the size of their audience. This will include the traffic that comes in and out of their Instagram accounts and their other pages. What you want is an influencer that not only commands a large audience but targets roughly the same demographics as you.

C. **Always Scrutinize**

The last thing you would want to take a look at is the general manner of which these people conduct themselves online. As such, there are several aspects that you need to take a look at which include:

1. Frequency - What is the volume of content that this influencer makes over a period of time? Are they always online or show up at the right time? Do they have a consistent content creation schedule?

There are a number of content creators and influencers out there that can post more than 20 Instagram status updates per day and then there are those that post only once a day or a week. Of course, it's not just the quantity of their content but quality. Some that post content once a day might net engagements by the millions of likes and comments per post.

2. Focus - Some influencers do well covering one certain topic while others can get all over the place but still generate a lot of traffic. The requirement on this part is rather simple: make sure that that influencer covers more than 30% of the topics that your brand also covers, at the very least.

3. Tone - This will cover their overall style as an influencer. Some are upbeat and perky. Others are cynical and abrasive. Some revel in being diplomatic and philosophical while others embrace controversy and are in your face with their demeanor.

4. Language - This does not exactly cover their preferred language I.e. English, French, or German, etc. What this does cover, however, is how they communicate with their audience. Influencers who cuss a lot, for instance, might generate a following with younger and brasher folk but might be off-putting for older demographics.

Also, this might be due to generational gaps. There are a lot of Gen-Xers and Baby Boomers out there that do not know who Ariane Grande is and those that do might or might not find her personality appealing.

In addition, find out if their style of language matches yours. Your brand might be comfortable with talking to your audience in a polite and professional way. As such, look for an influencer that does the same for your audience.

What you have to remember is that dealing with other people in the Internet is a hit-or-miss affair. Even the best collaborations can fall apart unless you know how to deal with your collaborators in a way that both of you can benefit from the relationship.

Also, influencers can only do so much. It you that has to do the heavy lifting as far as your native advertising is concerned. This means that you also have to engage with people regularly if you want to be as visible in your market as possible.

To Conclude

Social media marketing, as a whole, is a never-ending process. When looking at the success of your Instagram account's efforts to reach your target audience, there are two things that you need to consider.

First, is your brand listening to the larger conversation? The things that the Instagram community cares for as a whole do change from time to time. What may be relevant to your business now may not be appreciated that well by the rest of the Instagrammers.

That is, of course, if you insist on saying things the way that you want them to be said. There are ways of conveying messages that you care about while making sure that they are relevant to the rest of your audience. Just keep in mind that you pay attention to what other niches in your ever-growing audience cares for to keep your content relevant on the platform.

Second, what is quality of the content that you make? How well does it stack up against your competitors? Do your target audience even engage with it the moment that you post it?

The questions are answered if you take the time to understand what your analytics are saying to you. You need to know the trends that your content is following and compare them to how your competitors are faring. Perhaps the path to improvement lies in you understanding the strengths and weaknesses of your marketing, and that of others.

Chapter 5: Using Instagram Stories to Build Your Brand

The Stories feature is one of the more recent additions to Instagram and it has undoubtedly added a new twist to how things are being shared on the site. Initially released to compete with Snapchat, Instagram stories now has a lot of features which makes Instagram less of a glorified photo album and more of a viable marketing tool.

Integrating Instagram Stories for your marketing campaigns, then, could help instill loyalty to your customer base while also keeping the brand engaged with them.

Why Bother With Stories In The First Place?

As with all new features out there, the first thing that you might ask is why you should even consider Instagram Stories for your marketing efforts. The short answer is that stories offer a quick and engaging format, which makes it perfect for mobile users.

Also, there is the fact that popular brands have taken notice of the feature and a third of Instagram Stories now are generated by businesses and other large entities.

To put it in even simpler terms, Instagram stories are fun to go through or create and provides an unintimidating method for customers to reach out to the brands that they like the most. It offers a unique sense of authenticity that would otherwise take years and thousands of dollars to build in conventional online marketing strategies.

If that was not enough, here are several more facts that would make Instagram Stories a viable marketing tool:

1. User Base - As of now, Instagram Stories is reportedly use by 400 million users on a daily basis. That is 400 million opportunities for authentic engagement.

2. Minimal Effort - Stores have a short lifespan of 24 hours. Once that time has elapsed, whatever you post will be gone.

As such, you don't have to exert maximum mental effort to create stories and still get tons of engagement for your posts.

3. Experimentation - Typically, Instagram Stories are not segregated with the rest of the content being produced on the site. This means that you have the opportunity to test new campaigns here to see how well they can get engaged with in their 24-hour lifespan.

If something you post there receives a ton of likes and shares, then you can always migrate it to the more permanent form of your regular Instagram content. If it does not, well, it will be forgotten in a mere few hours with no costs on your part.

4. Traffic - Stories are quite integrated to Instagram's basic features which allows you to drive even more traffic to your main page and other marketing channels. You can add links to your Stories or advertise products that you may have on offer on Instagram's shop.

And then there is Instagram's Explore feature which allows your products to be easily discovered. If you are creative enough, you can even find ways to promote your other content from other social media accounts through the Stories feature.

How To Use Stories

So it's settled that the Stories feature has quite a lot to offer to marketers. The question is how you can use it to maximize your results? Again, its up to you how you can use Stories for your marketing but there are several surefire ways to integrate the feature to your campaign. Here are some of them:

1. Tutorials

This is the simplest and most direct method that you can use to take advantage of the stories feature. Tutorials can be short how-to videos or articles regarding the use of your products or services. Alternatively, you can use Stories for in-depth, multi-post content like product demonstrations and comparisons.

Either way, there is something about Stories that makes it the perfect place to put you more informational content in. For example, Delish dedicated their entire Stories page for posting of recipes on a daily basis. Also, Sephora used theirs to teach their customers how to make good use of the products that they offer.

Perhaps you are a tourism business. You can use the Stories feature to provide daily tips on travelling or feature some of the hotspots for certain cities and countries that you offer travel packages at. Or perhaps you own a restaurant or bar. You can use the stories feature to highlight the history of your signature dishes or give recipes so people can replicate the dishes themselves (without giving away your trade secrets, of course).

2. User Generated Content

There is nothing more persuasive and authentic as marketing content out there than the ones that are made by your own customers. The reason for this is that User-Generated Content accurately reflect the feelings and opinions that customers have regarding what you offer.

And since it is authentic and made by people who have direct experience with what you have to offer, they offer a more compelling sales pitch than whatever marketing strategy that you can come up with. This is why reviews on Yelp can make or break a restaurant's reputation. This is why movies can make a killing or fail spectacularly based on their ratings at sites like Rotten Tomatoes.

For Instagram, you can use content made by your customers to sell your own business in a number of ways. For instance, gyms can use the before and after pics of their members to convince people that their fitness regimes work.

For clothing brands, they can share pics of their customers wearing the products that they offer. And it makes for a far more convincing selling point for average folk than if a runway model does it.

And, for restaurants, they can always share the pictures of people dining into their dishes or having a good time at the place.

Aside from visual content, you can also share screenshots of reviews and testimonials made by people on review sites like Yelp or on Facebook on your Instagram account.

3. Behind-the-Scenes Looks

After that major plot twist in The Wizard of Oz, people have developed a seeming interest for what goes behind the public image that celebrities and businesses project in the market. You can use this to your advantage by giving people a peek behind the people that make up your business.

Use the Stories feature to let viewers see what a day in the life of your business looks like. Perhaps it could be you doing something on your desk or your staff creating the products or managing the services that your brand offers.

Either way, this well help in "humanizing" your brand as people now have a face to make an emotional connection with in regards to your business.

Movie studios often do this on Instagram by posting pictures of launch events or the goings-on in their movie sets. Even celebrities do this by posting pics of them relaxing with their families or staying at home doing nothing.

By showing that there are regular people that compose your business, you give the impression to your audience that your brand knows what it feels like to be human and thus can provide for basic human needs.

4. Polls and Quizzes

One neat feature in Instagram Stories is the ability to put up polls for your audience to interact with. Aside from the fact that polls are interactive by design, they also give you an insight as to what people care about the most which you could use for your marketing campaigns in the future. So it's an interactive campaign and market research scheme all rolled into one.

Putting up a quiz or poll is generally easy. You could use general information from the market or even trivia coming from your own brand. However, do not forget to add one last element which is the CTA at the end of the poll. Something like "Swipe to Finish" which leads to a separate business page is bound to increase conversions coming from this kind of content.

5. Special Announcements

If you want to add an element of prestige in your promotions, you can always use Stories to get your announcements across. For example, you may announce a special sale on Stories or announce a new set of products there.

As people go through the story, they may encounter an option like "Swipe to Link" or "Swipe to Shop". This will then take them to a separate page where they can get discounts for their purchases or better yet, get a hold of whatever you are trying to launch days in advance.

It brings a sense of belongingness and accomplishment to your customers, knowing that they got hold of something sweet since they made the effort to interact with your story.

6. Customer Feedback

Aside from polls and quizzes, you can also host live Question and Answer sessions on Instagram Stories. This should provide your audience the opportunity to directly interact with you while having their questions answered. It is something similar to Reddit's Ask Me Anything feature but a bit less text-based.

However, do keep in mind that how you answer questions will ultimately determine whether or not this tactic works for you in Instagram's stories.

When the videogame company Electronic Arts launched an Ask Me Anything session on Reddit regarding issues about their game Star Wars: Battlefront II, they botch every question by giving every answer a Public Relations and Marketing tone. And then there was their answer to lootboxes which they claim gives players a "sense of Pride and Accomplishment".

Needless to say, an opportunity to fix their relations with their customer base further drove the wedge while the Pride and Accomplishment answer was entered into the Guinness World Book of Records as the most downvoted Internet comment in History.

7. Limited Time Offers

There is nothing that make people convert faster than being on a sense of Urgency. This is why limited offers worked so much in conventional advertising and still does even in Social Media today. Instagram stories have a 24-hour lifespan which makes them the perfect home for your limited offers.

For instance, you can make an announcement there about a sale which leads to a separate page where people can get a discount code. As such, only those that have interacted with the story while it is still posted can get a hold of the discount.

How to Improve Your Stories' Performance

There is a difference between posting stories and making them actually effective. Anybody can post a story on Instagram but it takes a lot of care to create one that not only engages with your audience but would actually compel them to do something mutually beneficial for the brand and the person.

To do this, there are a few tips to keep in mind when creating your Story.

1. Put Interaction at the Forefront Always

The kind of story you put up determines the level of interaction it will generate. For instance, Q and A sessions are designed to be highly interactive along with polls, swipe to link schemes, and even overlay text.

Of course, there are the challenges which directly tap into a person's primal competitiveness. Use hashtag challenges along with swipe to links, limited offers, and other gamified content to make your content even more engaging to your audience.

2. Highlight

The 24-hour lifespan of Stories can be both a problem and a benefit for your business. It's good that you don't have to exert a lot of effort in pushing your content in stories but you run the risk of losing what is a practically good Story in just a day.

By using the Highlight feature, you can extend the life of your best-engaged stories by a few days or more. Not only will this extend their lifespan but would also neatly categorize your content. Now, you can know which of your stories are generating a lot of engagement and which are not.

3. Run a Story Ad

It's often been told that Instagram Stories get 5 times more engagement than regular Instagram content. As such, the feature makes for a good place to run your advertisements on. And keep in mind that not a lot of brands are not doing this (yet) which means you can still take advantage of the small population of advertisements there.

4. Work with Influencers

As was previously stated, working with the right collaborator can be beneficial to your Instagram campaign. For stories, working with a collaborator gives you access to certain perks like product reviews, cost-effective promotions, and a smaller rate of customer acquisition cost.

And with Stories, the exposure is beneficial to both you and your influencer of choice. They get to closely interact with their fans while naturally pointing the same fans to your products which should increase conversion rates while also expanding your presence in the market.

5. Get Creative

There are a lot of features on offer in Stories that would make your stories even more attractive. Things like emojis, moving graphics, filter, and video editing features can enhance your text and visuals.

But, of course, there is a fine line between adding enhancements to your text and visuals and flooding your stories with too many distractions. Just use the right enhancements to get your point across so you don't lose your audiences in the confusion.

6. Never Underestimate the Power of Tagging

Tags are there to make your content even easier to discover by potential audiences. For example, Geotags help audiences discover where you are mainly operating at or where you are currently located. This will also link your brand to nearby tourist attractions, major events and hotspots, driving traffic to your page.

Hashtags, on the other hand, can make your content relevant to whatever is currently happening across the world. When the Duke and Duchess of Cambridge tied the knot, Lego did a series of campaigns based on the Royal

Wedding with the appropriate tags. This enabled their campaign to be part of the conversation; more importantly, it was linked to an event that everybody else is talking about.

The Main Takeaway

When all is said and done, what you have to understand is that there are many ways to push a story. The strategy that you will use depends greatly on the type of business that you have and the customers you are trying to target.

As such, it is best that you try out a few approaches and experiment with your content if the budget allows for it. Over time, you should be able to find a content that is highly interactive that your brand can use repeatedly in the future.

Lead Generation With Stories

In all of these campaigns, what you have to remember is that your end goal is to generate leads which subsequently generates sales. If your campaigns are not impacting the bottom line of the brand, then there's no point doing it in the first place.

So how do all these campaigns lead to sales? If you include links to your web content, of course.

The new Swipe Up feature should take your audiences from the story to a page of yours which should nudge people one step further into completing the conversion process.

To generate sales and leads for your Instagram Stories, there are a few things that you need to keep in mind.

1. Share Your Web Content

As was stated, Content is the King of online marketing strategies. Good content is essential for a good SEO ranking and in generating and nurturing leads.

With Instagram stories, you can share a relevant photo or other similar content and then add a link to that which takes audiences to various pages that you own. That page may be a blog, or an ebook, or even your YouTube channel.

The point is that Instagram Stories can consolidate the traffic coming through your different web channels which, in theory, should increase the chances of people converting into paying customers.

Also, you can use stories to promote sales and special events as more than 30% of Instagram users have been known to purchase a product based on what they saw on their IG feeds. Keep in mind that social media can influence the purchasing decisions of people today so it makes sense to do a lot of visual-based marketing there.

Target, for example, uses their Instagram account to specifically target impulse buyers. By constantly showcasing whatever is new in their product line at Instagram and then following that with the Swipe Up button that leads to a sales page, Target has hastened the purchasing decisions of these kinds of buyers.

Of course, this results in faster conversions in an already fast-paced buyer base.

2. Make Influencers Your Ambassadors

Going back to influencers, we have already talked about how effective they are in pushing your products and services without being too "pushy" with their own audiences. Also, they already have sizeable followings which may become your potential customers with the right kind of messages.

But there is one more element that you have to consider with influencers as far as Instagram Stories and concerned and that is how you treat them. In other marketing, it is enough that they are your collaborators. In Instagram Stories, however, they become your Ambassadors.

What's the difference, then? A normal messenger may push the product and service but an Ambassador does way more than that.

More often than not, they can sell the brand to their audience and that includes everything from the products, services, and even the lifestyle associated with your business. They may even come up with ways to how make better use of your offerings which adds another dimension to the way your business is being treated by the rest of the market.

If people see that a person that they can interact with is doing great using your products, then they are less hesitant to make the conversion themselves. And consider the fact that Influencer-sourced leads often have higher chances of becoming customers themselves.

3. Respond Directly

One of the direct results of becoming more active in Instagram Stories is the increase of direct messages coming your way. If a story of yours does not include a link, users will be able to see a message bar. Using this, they can directly message your account for all sorts of queries and concerns.

While this is a feature that can easily bridge the gap between a brand and its audience/followers, it can be detrimental to your business if you choose to ignore DMS entirely. If you are not quick enough to answer a question, that potential audience may get tired and look elsewhere for someone to meet their needs.

This is why it is important for marketers to not just focus on sticking to the script that they have planned for the campaign. They must be quick enough to address any issue raised by their audience, legitimate or otherwise.

To Wrap Things Up...

Understanding how Instagram Stories work and what you can gain from it is just the first half of a rather elaborate solution. With a rather unique storytelling concept and a strong potential for conversion, how you actually use the Stories feature as a marketing tool will determine how your campaign in that page will be effective.

What you must not forget is to constantly engage with your fans there and be consistent enough in providing them with something to consume. The more you give value to your audience there, the quicker conversion rates will be for your brand on the platform as a whole.

But entertaining people is not just your end goal in marketing. You have to give them something tangible in order to give them that final push towards conversion. And, luckily enough for you, Instagram does have a page dedicated to everything related to products.

Chapter 6: Shopping in Instagram

In recent years, Instagram has been slowly veering away from its purely Social Media concept. In fact, the site has been trying its luck with ecommerce with its new Shop feature.

Again, with all things, you can choose to ignore this feature entirely for your marketing campaigns. But, if you think about it more, why would you?

Instagram has been relentless in updating the feature and a standalone app is already in the works. What is clear that ecommerce is becoming an important part of Instagram and, as far as you are concerned, a viable marketing tool for your business.

What's an Instagram Shop, Exactly?

The best way to describe the Shop page is that it combines your Instagram profile with a standard product catalogue. As such, the Shop allows you to directly promote your products to your audiences through posts, Stories, and every other page on Instagram.

In essence, you are setting up a mini version of your main website at Instagram where people can go into and hopefully complete the customer conversion process. The page is also quite helpful as it provides potential buyers with a lot of information including:

- Product Name

- Images

- Description of the Product

- Price

- A link that leads to your main website for further details (or to complete the ordering process there)

- Other products related or similar to it

Benefits

Instagram's venture into ecommerce has been lauded by industry experts and small online businesses alike. But what does choosing to set up shop on Instagram bring to you compared to, say, Amazon? Here are some 3 distinct advantages.

1. It Reduces Noise

With a lot of businesses vying the attention of the same group of people, it can get difficult at times to even compel potential buyers to drop whatever they are currently doing and visit your store.

So, if you can't get them to go to your store, what's the alternative? YOU take your store to THEM. On Instagram Shop, casual viewers can go to your shop and check on the prices without being taken away from the main site. Plus, if they think that they are ready to make a purchase, they can start a transaction with just one push of the button.

This non-intimidating and simple concept can be enough to encourage people to take a look at what you have to offer while casually scrolling through the main Instagram feed.

2. Direct Promotion

One of the major drawbacks to Instagram has always been its linking feature. In fact, to this day, you are only allowed one link at your main profile and you can't add clickable links to any of the content that you post.

As such, it was such a chore to directly promote products on the platform especially if you already have a sizeable catalog of things to sell. This one-link-only scheme can even hurt conversion rates as you are only allowed to direct your potential buyers to one page which could be lost if ever you update your bio.

This is where the Instagram Shop comes into play as it allows you to integrate all of your Instagram marketing campaigns with the store itself. So, if you have something to promote, you can directly lead your audiences to the Shop page which speeds up the conversion process. It also reduces the chances of people tuning off your marketing since they now have somewhere to go to in order to check the things that you have to offer.

Lastly, navigating from the main Instagram feed to Shop page and back is quite simple and easy to understand.

3. Massive Exposure

Every product that you post on Instagram's Shop would be included in the new Shopping Explore tab. On paper, this should increase engagement with your brand provided that you optimize the hashtags of each of your entries.

Also, the Explore tab is unique for each and every user as it is put up based on their activity on the site as well as their interests. As such, the things that would appear on every person's Explore tab is bound to be made up of things that they may take a liking to.

The end result is that your products will be exposed to an audience with an already high purchase intent insofar as the type of products you are selling are concerned. To put it in other words, customer conversion rates are higher on the shop as the target audience there are likely going to buy whatever you have to offer.

To put it even simpler terms, the Shop is a powerful tool that can boost sales for your products quickly. That is, of course, if you set things up properly.

How to Set Up Shop

Before anything else, you have to understand that the Shop option is only available for now if you set up your profile as a Business. As such, if your profile is Private for now, you may have to set up a separate account for your business and shop.

There are also other ways to set the shop up via Syncing with pages like a Facebook Shop page or a Shopify account. If you have either, you can automatically sync your Instagram Shop with them which copies and migrates all your data from there to your new page. As for the Facebook page sync, Instagram will ask an extra requirement of you being the admin of that page before they allow the link.

But whether or not you have an existing Shop page or not, there are three steps that you must take in putting up an Instagram Shopping tab.

1. Read the Rules

Instagram has a handful of requirements that would be shopkeepers should meet before they are allowed to promote their business at the page. First, the Shop page is not for the selling of services, only products i.e. physical goods.

Next, Instagram has set up a list of commerce policies that shop owners should adhere to. Violations of one or multiple stipulations on a frequent basis might lead to the termination of your Shop page or, worse, your entire account.

Third, your business must be located in a country with access to the feature. Instagram has a list of countries where the Instagram Shop feature is currently available. You better hope that your country is included there if you want to set the shop up.

Finally, you must make sure that your version of Instagram is up to date. Fortunately, updating the site or the app will take only a few minutes, downloading and installation included.

2. Building the Catalog

It is here that having a Facebook Shop would come in handy as Instagram tends to pull off information from its sister site when creating your catalog. There are several options on the catalog page of which sites you can link up to such as Facebook and Shopify. Just click on those two options and your Instagram catalog should be set up in a few minutes.

Once you are confident that your product catalog is decently organized, the last thing you want to click is the "Make Products Available" option. This should allow Instagram to start promoting your products at the Explore pages of your target demographics.

3. Setting up the Sales Channel

This part is dependent on the fact that you have a Shopify account. To set up the channel, all you have to do is to go to your Shopify Dashboard and click on the available sales channels there.

You should see your Instagram profile as one of the options there. Just click on the + icon which directly connects your IG profile to the Shopify page. This means that any person who wishes to purchase a product of their liking will be taken there.

Of course, you can also link your IG profile to the sales channel in your main website. This should increase the traffic from your IG profile and main website and consolidate all of your transactions.

4. Wait for Approval

At this point, you should have done the following:

- Set up an Instagram Business profile

- Linked the profile to Facebook Shop and Shopify

- Synced your product catalogs in other sites with your Instagram page.

- Linked your main website to the Instagram shop.

Once you have done all of this, Instagram's administrators will then review your account which could take a few hours or a few days.

If you do get approved, you will get a notification that tells you of such.

5. Get Started

Upon receiving that notification, what you will have to do next is to confirm which of your shops that you would want to connect with your Instagram profile. You should click on the Get Started option at the Business settings and select the Shopping option.

Next, you will then have to select the different shops you have currently available. Doing so will sync all your product catalogs into one.

However, there may be an off-chance that your product would not be neatly organize upon assembly or there will be duplicate entries for the same product. This happens regularly if you source your info from multiple sources. Fortunately, you can sort and take out the entries that you do not like and create subcategories for similar products.

Either way, Your Instagram Shop is now good to go.

All that is left to do is to tag your products in each of your posts as well as your content on the Stories page. In fact, you can tag as much as 20 products in multi-image posts or at least 5 for singular image posts.

However, just keep in mind that your Shop page can only be fully activated upon the posting of your first Shop post.

The Main Takeaway:

At a glance, you could already get the notion that setting up your Shop at Instagram can get a hassle especially if you are not that tech-savvy. You are not exactly creating an independent shop page but one that syncs itself to whatever existing shop page you have on other sites.

But if you do this right, you should be able to put up a page that is easy to navigate through and is automatically promoted on Instagram's Shopping Explore feature. All that is left to do now is to make sure that you have enough products to sell in your different sales channels.

Remarketing and How It is Done

The word "remarketing" might sound like an intimidating marketing term but it's actually quite a simple concept.

Let us assume that you have over 50,000 followers after several months on Instagram. That size is something considerable for a mid-sized business. However, would you believe that the number of people who follow you and actually find your products to be interesting does not even reach 10%? Most of them just find your marketing campaigns neat and not much else, while others just stumbled on your profile by accident.

With that volume of people going to your Shop page, main profile, and main website, wouldn't it make sense to retarget them with your offers? That is the very concept of remarketing and, to do this, you have to identify the kind of people that interact with your brand. They usually fall under 3 categories.

- **Buyers -** These people are the ones that need the least convincing as they already had purchased your products before. The best thing that you can do with the people is to entice with the another, better offer and hope that they would take you up on your offer.

  For example, you might be a clothing store and a lot of people purchased a certain item from your Shop a few months ago. You can retarget those people with an offer for a "version 2" of that shirt or something that goes along well with it. The point is that   you should give them a good reason to buy something from you again.

- **Cart Bailers -** These are the people that actually went through the effort of converting into customers but just missed the final part: parting with their money. These people have already placed something on their carts or their favorites list but did not actually purchase them for one reason or another.

  You can place these people on a separate list but are actually easy enough to remarket. After all, they already have shown interest for your product. They only failed to take action on those interest or even follow through with their purchases.

- **Browsers -** These are the people that actually went through your Shop but did not do anything particularly noteworthy there. They didn't like any of your offers and did not do anything remotely close to starting a transaction with the page.

Remarketing these people can a bit more effort as you still have to convince them that whatever you are offering is something of value. However, you can make this easier on your part by putting these browsers into one group and creating a more labor-intensive marketing campaign that exclusively targets them in the future.

So once you have identified the kind of people going through your Shop page, how do you actually go about remarketing them? There are a number of strategies that you can use, depending on the kind of people that you want to retarget. However, in order to make any of your strategies effective, there are several things that you have to remember.

1. Start with Top Performers

Are you familiar with the term "low hanging fruit"? This is a kind of marketing where you do minimal effort for maximum effect. In the case of remarketing, this involves going back to the campaigns that net you a lot of engagements and reintroducing them to the market, with updates of course.

The reason for this simple: that campaign had a lot of potential to convert more people. What if it can yield you more if you reintroduce it in the market? This strategy is not exactly frowned upon in marketing as remarketing does get expensive especially with Google's AdWords feature.

Once you are sure that you have wrung out every extra bit of conversion you can get from these campaigns, you can then move on to newer ones.

2. Maximum Effort Counts, Too

Although click-through rates tend to drop in time with remarketing, studies do show that conversion is more certain with these ads especially in shoppers who are familiar with the brand.

As such, it is recommended that you do not hesitate to spend a bit more or get a bit more creative when it comes to your remarketing schemes. Think of it this way: the people you are marketing already know what your products are and have already expressed their interest for the brand. As such, the chances of experiencing better conversions from these people are higher as well as reduced marketing costs for every successful sale.

3. Be Careful with Your Keywords and Tags

Anyone who has ever done SEO that broad keywords are generally avoided. This is because they only work well in funneling a lot of traffic and not much else.

However, conversion has already occurred partly or totally in remarketing. As such, broader keywords and tags will help you on this matter. Also, it helps that broad keywords and tags are cheaper too which means that you can get a ton of conversion for a fraction of your initial marketing costs.

4. Special Offers are the Key

This strategy works well with those that bailed on their purchases. The reason is that these people already displayed interest for the brand but did not follow through the sales process for one reason or another.

With remarketing, you can target these people by offering something even better than what they initially planned to purchase a while ago.

Be it a bundle, a special discount for returning audiences, or an entirely new item, whatever could sweeten the deal can help in bringing these potential customers back to the fold.

5. Be Frequent but Don't be Annoying

As with all things, remarketing only works well if you don't overdo it. A shopper will find it annoying if you bombard them with the same ad again and again to the point that they would tune you. This is regardless of how good your offers actually are.

If possible, do time your remarketing efforts so much so that they are evenly spaced one ad from the other. The duration of how long an ad should be followed with another should not be too long that people forget what you were offering them and not too short that it becomes a daily occurrence. And do remember that spamming messages has never worked well in the Internet.

To Wrap Things Up...

So, is Instagram's Shop page completely necessary to make your marketing campaigns there work? Not really. The feature still has a lot of kinks to work out and there is the fact that putting it up in the first place is quite tedious.

However, that does not mean that the feature does not pose some advantages to brands as far as their sales are concerned. Remember that the end goal of marketing is always the business's bottom line. And since the Shop feature does directly affect that, it is best that you take the time to learn what it can offer for your business and whether or not your staff can keep up with its rather strict demands.

Chapter 7: Appealing to Generation Z

As of now, the most relevant market to target are the Millennials. This is because they have the right combination of youth, activity, and purchasing power which makes them a potent segment to focus on, especially on Instagram. But, just as with any generation, they would soon be replaced with a far more potent generation to market to.

Born during the late 1990s, right at the formative years of the Internet Age, Generation Z is a highly cautious and tech-savvy generation. With almost all of them finally acquiring purchasing power, they are already playing a valuable role on how marketing is done especially in the online world.

However, there are challenges to face when marketing to these individuals. Their high affinity towards technology and access to a trove of information makes them difficult to market to if you insist on using traditional forms of marketing. In fact, many predict that Gen Z folk would require a different approach altogether compared to the generation that directly preceded them.

There is one thing that you should remember about this market and that is the fact that Social Media has a huge presence in their lives. As such, you have to learn how to use that dependence to your advantage in creating campaigns that they will engage with. Besides, many of the insights that apply to this group also apply to many millennials, so you might want to take note.

What Makes Gen Z a Challenge to Market To?

Since they were born right at the dawn of the Internet Age, Gen Z folk have a stronger connection to online technology than older age groups. This strong affinity, in turn, has brought about some distinct behaviors in them as far their treatment with marketing messages are concerned.

If you insist on making the Gen Z people a core group to market to, there are some notable behaviors that you should be aware of which include the following:

1. They Don't Give a Damn About Brand Loyalty

In traditional marketing, the way the message is form revolves around telling the rest of the world that your brand is the best out there for certain conditions or the best out there period. For Gen Z people, however, such kind of marketing is seen as pushy, abrasive, and noisy.

If you are used to the notion that you can drown the rest of the market by making a lot more noise through your marketing, you can be certain that Gen Z folk are going to tune you out. They won't convert and become loyal to you and they can access information on the Internet to stand by their convictions.

In essence, they won't take the bait if all that you are saying is that your products or services are good. However, what they do look for are businesses that can provide solutions to problems that they constantly face.

For example, Gen Zs don't shop at certain clothing brands because they offer cheap prices or they use high-end materials for their products. They do so because the designs are hip and cute which helps them with their image (a problem that they often deal with on a daily basis given their age range and how society functions in recent years).

To target these people to become paying customers, then, you have to offer ideas and solutions to whatever issue that resonates with Gen Z people the most. The more effective that solution is, the more recognizable that brand will be to this age group.

2. Marketing is in a Free For All Now

Back then, it was the norm that the competition you have to take seriously are the brands that offer the same products and services as you. Or, alternatively, it is those companies that target the same demographics as you.

However, given the higher level of consumer agency being afforded by Gen Z folk today, competition for any kind of business comes in various shapes, sizes, and business types.

In most cases, the competition that you have to seriously consider now comes not from big-time businesses and key industry players but from smaller businesses and brands. For instance, a deli today does not have to deal with other delis but also fusion cafes and bakeries that offer artisanal meal options for Gen Zers who want more quality for a fraction of the cost.

The reason why smaller companies are becoming a larger threat today is for the fact that they are closer in proximity to the markets that they operate in. By virtue of being closer, they can better engage with their target markets and Gen Z people are all about businesses that show their humanity nowadays.

Also, you should consider the fact that this group hates Information Overload. If they are exposed to the same kind of marketing message on a day to day basis, no matter how good it is, they will tune it out and ignore such brands for the rest of the foreseeable future.

3. They Care For More Things Than the Bottom Line

In a twist that would make every hardcore capitalist out there shake to their boots, marketing today has been forced to take an angle of selflessness. No, this does not mean that businesses have abandoned their purely capitalist roots since the name of the game is still about making money.

However, what this means is that businesses today are compelled by Generation Z people to consider other forms of capital to remain sustainable in their markets. Things like Altruism, care for the environment, community relations, and other feel-good ideas out there can make people gravitate towards your brand.

Remember that marketing today is all about giving value. So what better value is out there right now than signaling to the rest of the Gen Z market that you care for the same things that they care about?

Of course, this does pose some problems. Brands that opt to focus on social issues must not forget that they need to secure their bottom lines first. And keep in mind that Gen Z people are generally more wary of businesses attempting to reach out to them.

If your move towards becoming more socially aware is generally viewed as insincere and pandering, there is a chance that you will not only get the support of the Gen Z people but you will also alienate other generations who are not too keen with businesses suddenly becoming all too preachy with their marketing.

This is what happened when Gillette decided to make their official stance known in issues like Feminism and the #MeToo Movement. Although it can be seen that their goal was noble i.e. to reach out to a comparatively smaller demographic, the way they handled their messaging was botched as it looked like they were attacking their primary customer base which were men.

In the end, Proctor and Gamble had to deal with an $8 Billion write down for Gillette and had to do a major refocusing of their marketing in the latter half of 2019.

As the saying goes right now: if you choose to "Get Woke", you open yourself up to the risk of getting broke.

4. **They Move Through Devices a Lot**

Gen Z people are born at a generation when technological dependency was it its highest. They also are the generation with the strongest access to multiple technological devices that it is no surprise that they would move from one device to another.

If Gen X folk have a hard time moving from one screen to another, Gen Z people can do five. Due to these constant leapfrogging between devices and social media platforms, the challenge now for marketers is to be able to predict what devices they often use the most and what platforms they have a strong preference for.

5. **They Are Bold with their Opinions**

Here's the thing with Generation Z people: if they think that your brand sucks or your marketing sucks, they will not hesitate to tell you. In your virtual face.

The reason for this is simple: these people where raised in a time when Personalization become a norm in marketing. Everything has to be tailor made to suit their needs. Combine this with their access to social media and you have an entire generation of people who are not afraid to express their love and disappointment for the things that they are exposed to.

Older generations would call this trend "bellyaching" but, for marketers, it is something that they could take advantage of. Also, for marketers, it is important to remember that criticisms from this age group counts as a valid form of social interaction so it is best to take what they say with a purely objective standpoint.

Why Instagram Plays a Huge Role with This Group

As of now, Instagram is one of the strongest platforms to operate on as far as Visual Branding is concerned. In fact, it is the one that caters the most to the sensibilities of the Gen Z people compared to Facebook and Twitter.

Due to its highly visual nature, Instagram is a natural pairing for brands that thrive on offering highly visual content. This includes Food Service, Fashion, Lifestyle, Travel, and Self-Help.

But this does not mean other businesses can't use the site as well. Financial services used to veer away from Instagram as the nature of their product was seen as incompatible with the format provided on Instagram.

This all changed in 2013 when PayPal launched a campaign there that depicted the lives of its users with a strong focus on how the services it offers makes the lives of people easier. Things like showing the ability to pay for your bills remotely or purchase things through their program might look simple at a glance but they did tap into the Gen Z's need for mobility and simplicity in their transactions.

In essence, by showing the lifestyle that is eventually reached with their product, and not the product per se, PayPal managed to secure a foothold in younger demographics who were starting to acquire their purchasing powers at that point of time. As far as analytics are concerned, PayPal's simple but ingenious campaign led to a 327% increase in audience engagement for that year alone.

Sadly, not all businesses are that clever and commit a grave mistake on Instagram which old-school marketers would call as "Preaching to the Choir". They create posts that target themselves instead of their followers and potential customers. Things like offering discounts, coupons, and announcements of sales are great but they are not that effective in reaching out to Generation Z audiences.

If you want to know if your messaging would work on Gen Z people on Instagram, there are a few questions that you need to answer as honestly as you could.

- Do these people use my products or services on a daily basis?

- In what way does your offer improve the quality of their life?

- In what way does your brand lend a hand in making their world a better place?

The way you answer these questions might even lead you to improving your core marketing message which should aid in generating interest for your brand in your people and, of course, starting a conversation with them. Then you should consider refining the way you present your messages in a manner that makes it more personal and human to this young audience group.

Why Videos Matter More Now And How To Do Video Marketing On Instragram

The introduction of features like Instagram TV and Facebook Live only further cements the notion that video has a place in the years to come as a marketing tool. In fact, studies revealed that demographics coming from the younger generations can watch as much as 86 videos per day of varying lengths.

How can anyone take advantage of this rising trend? The answer is on investing on good video content and the right distribution channel. Videos, by themselves, can be used to create an entirely unique brand persona while entertaining or educating audiences. If done right, it could even yield a lot of engagement from a lot of demographics.

In order to set up a potent video content campaign on Instagram, there are a few steps that you need to follow.

1. Find the Right Messenger (and Message)

First and foremost, your brand has to invest in a person with a personality good enough to carry the marketing message in your video. This is quite important especially if you are going to use the TV feature for content like tutorials, webinars, and product demonstrations.

When it comes to targeting younger demographics, you also need to know a few things about your audience like:

- How do they talk?

- What interests them?

- What issues do they care about the most?

- What don't they like in general?

As for the message, you must remember that Gen Z people care a lot about social issues which you can use to your advantage. Ben and Jerry's video channels on YouTube and Instagram, for example, have videos that talk about things like gender equality, climate change, and freedom of speech.

By giving the impression that they want to start a conversation with social issues, the brand managed to establish a strong and loyal following in younger people in the recent years.

2. Be Authentic as Possible

Due to the constant connection to the internet and overexposure to all kinds of marketing, Gen Z people tend to a lot more skilled in detecting insincere marketing than older generations. If they feel that brands are approaching not because they want to establish a personal connection but to purely earn from their purchases, younger audiences can and will ignore that brand for as long as humanly possible.

Also, people nowadays don't like to be talked down to or being pandered to. For them, these can cheapen the value of the things that they care about if a blatant marketing tone is laid on top of it. Being transparent, on the other hand, tends to be more acceptable for these people.

If you can't muster an interest in social issues or choose to be neutral with certain issues, then the best that you can do is to be as honest as possible about it. It would be more effective to strive for a more authentic image than to shoehorn a political or social issue to your marketing.

If your brand wants to support a cause, on the other hand, it must be able to draw a parallel between that cause and its own values. For example, if a restaurant claims to support environmental issues, then it should be seen in its practices like how it sources food, to the kind of utensils they provide (e.g. straw, plastic spoons) to how it even disposes its waste.

The point is that being authentic as possible tends to make people care about your brand more. In Instagram, the ability to show authenticity (as opposed to merely talking about it) should net you a lot of support from younger people.

3. Make it Mobile Friendly

There are three particular reasons why you should optimize your videos for mobile platforms. First, a third of the entire population of Internet users today access the online market through their mobile devices. Second, videos are one of the most shared contents out there at 92% more than text and images.

Third, and exclusive to Gen Z folk, almost all of them have a mobile device now. So how do you make your videos mobile optimized?

The first thing to do is to keep it short. Videos that have longer watch times are harder to share as younger demographics are often intimidated by anything that goes beyond the 20 minute mark. The 5 minute mark is good but you can also aim for 10 minutes depending on the subject you are tackling.

Next, pack every minute with actionable ideas. This is where a good messenger comes into play as they can turn otherwise boring ideas into something exciting and easy to process.

Other Important Strategies

As was previously mentioned, Gen Z people are a bit trickier to market to. However, that does not mean that they are next to impossible as potential marketing audiences. Here are several more strategies that you can use when interacting with this demographic.

1. Loyalty Through Interaction

Gen Z people might not be that particular with loyalty but they are actually more eager to interact with brands. Here are some specific data that you could use regarding Gen Z buying behavior:

- 42% would actually participate in online challenges and events that a brand might come up with.

- 38% are more likely to attend an event in the real world sponsored by an online brand.

- 44% have shown interest in helping brands improve on their products by submitting design ideas and propositions.

- 36% are more than willing to create user generated content that brands can use for their marketing provided that they ask for their consent first.

This means that you could use some older forms of online marketing for these people. This includes challenges, polls, quizzes, and even customer feedback. They are even less hesitant to brands whose Instagram profiles also reply to their comments.

The more you interact with these people, the more likely it is that they would consume whatever you have to offer. But the manner of your interactions would also matter which leads to the next point which is...

2. Understand How they Use Social Media

Even if Social Media sites are designed to cater to all people, the way that each person uses it is different from one another. As far as Gen Z people are concerned, Instagram is used for two things only: to express themselves and to discover the hippest and trendiest brands in the market.

Your marketing should focus on the latter by keeping up with what people care about these days. Whether they are the newest superfoods or the most recent progressive issues, your brand must find a way to incorporate these messages in order to tap into younger demographics.

For example, GoPro found out that its target demographics are into engaging or sharing videos of people extreme sports on social media. Thus, they came up with a brilliant marketing campaign that highlighted people engaging in dangerous and thrilling scenarios which includes firemen going through a burning building or thrill-seekers jumping off cliffs. It was so effective that engagement for GoPro's social media profiles rose up to 300% for that campaign's entire period.

3. Make Privacy a Point

Out of all the marketing generations, it is the Gen Z people that are most protective of their privacy. In essence, they want to make sure that whatever happens in the Internet, stays on the Internet. As such, they are less likely to share their personal information for brands especially the ones that they don't trust.

Also, Gen Z people are more likely to gravitate towards spaces where their identities can remain safely private like Facebook's Messenger app or Snapchat. As such, it is ideal that you put a bit of emphasis on marketing for these private channels as the people there are less likely to resist whatever marketing message that you are trying to convey.

But you have to gain their trust first. This can be done through the aforementioned focus on transparency. Give them the assurance that whatever information that they will provide will not be used for any purpose that they did not consent to. Or, better yet, you could try to come up with marketing campaigns that are not overly reliant on asking the audience to cough up private information.

To Conclude

As of writing, it is the Generation Z people that marketers have the most issues with. They are technically unpredictable, prone to sudden shifts in mood, and are the loudest when expressing their opinion.

It also is important to note that these individuals are starting to acquire stronger purchasing powers which means that the effects that they would have on the market would just become potent in the next decade.

But, fortunately enough, this age group is still receptive to marketing messages, just not through the usual strategies that marketers are most comfortable. The ability to adapt your Instagram strategies to address what these people are looking for can become vital if your overall goal there is to expand your brand's reach towards segments that you have yet to tap into.

Chapter 8: Public Relations on Instagram

The way brands market themselves in the field of social media is always evolving. This means that new strategies are always cooked up every year to make businesses and individuals stand out more in places like Instagram. On the flip side, this means that it is harder to make an impact if you are comfortable with using the same strategy over and over for years on end.

But the one strategy that has remained timeless ever since has been Public Relations. The ability to create goodwill with your brand and maintain that is a skill that many find hard to pull off but remains a necessary asset for many business.

And since Instagram has evolve past its filtered photo album days and is a viable marketing tool, a good PR strategy will not only be more than welcome here but it might just ensure the brand remains visible in the market, and for all the right reasons.

The "Nice Guy" Approach Still Works

We have all heard phrases of how marketing is supposed to be cutthroat and everyone doing it has to be precise, relentless, and assertive. But there is a fine line between being an effective marketer and being that Hollywood stereotype of businessmen being pushy jocks in fancy suits.

The truth is that being the "nice guy" in marketing does yield a lot of results and most of them are ultimately beneficial to the business. This is why Public Relations as a strategy is tantamount to being that "nice guy". So how does one do it especially on Instagram? Here's How.

1. Collaborate, Not Compete

As was previously mentioned, changes in consumer behavior have turned marketing into a Free for Fall. Everyone is a potential competitor and cross-promotional schemes means that any brand can vie for the same people as others in the market.

Of course, being competitive is part of human nature. It's what allowed the Business world to thrive even in the age of distrusting consumers. But an effective business person and marketer does not have to butt heads with every other person there that does not share their brand.

Instead of being competitors, a "nice guy" marketer sees every business as a potential addition to their network. As such, they can tap into these businesses to meet a common goal instead of undermining them in every step of their campaign.

2. Being Diplomatic

There's no arguing that a lot of conflict starts with miscommunication. A business may say something seemingly innocent about their competitor which the latter would take as an offense. Of course, this is not to discount the fact that businesses have not been engaging in typical corporate trash talking for years or the fact that some business owners take criticism too personally.

In Public Relations, one of the essential skills you must learn is knowing what to say, when to say it, and how to say it. An understanding that marketing networks are volatile is a key skill here so it really pays to be the least toxic person in the market.

For instance, you might put out content on Instagram with the intention of congratulating a competitor. Your staff must find a way to say your message as sincerely as possible so the other group does not take your compliment as thinly-veiled sarcasm.

Or what if you just want to put out an announcement that your business is about to unveil a new product or service? You can do that without taking jabs at your competitors by mocking their previous campaigns.

Conversely, this means that the brand itself must be able to accept negative customer feedback and criticisms and thoroughly consider how you respond to such. The less conflict every move your brand generates, the more opportunities for networking and business will pop up.

3. Transparency

Bluffing and bluster used to be effective strategies in closing deals or saving face. There was this seeming fear to appear weak in front of a potential partner so marketers then used to make bold claims in the hopes that they don't get called out for it. Problems arise, however, if people do call you out on your bluff and find out that you not much to offer.

One important skill to master in Public Relations is the ability to tell the truth without needlessly compromising yourself. Things like the actual capabilities of the business or the product to its policies.

This is not about giving out information that would unnecessarily expose your business to people who might take advantage of your brand's weak points. It is just that you are better off not dealing with expectations that your brand could not meet.

4. Being Empathetic

Every marketing effort that says that your business cares for something would mean nothing if you don't show it. This goes beyond saying things that people like or standing up for causes that people right now care for.

In PR, there is a strong emphasis to make people feel that your brand sees them as actual human beings with legitimate needs and concerns that must be addressed. This is where a lot of brands fail with their PR and marketing as their efforts end too short that everything feels forced.

What you have to always remember is that people nowadays are more discerning as consumers. They can tell when a business is just trying to connect with them without offering something meaningful. And if they smell insincerity, they will not hesitate to call brands out for it.

5. Consistency

One particular reason why businesses do not enjoy a lot of trust from the public is their tendency to say one thing and do another. It's like when a videogame company promises not to put microtransactions in their games and do exactly just that or when a company claims that they care about their customers but take every opportunity to antagonize them on social media.

And this concerns not only customers and outside elements. There are instances when companies project an image of a healthy workplace and yet we hear reports of toxic work environments, employee abuse, and worse. In both instances, the point is that being inconsistent can be detrimental to the reputation of a brand.

Good PR, then, is about practicing the old saying "practice what you preach". If you project an image of approachability on Instagram, then it must be seen in the way your staff deals with customers, suppliers, and even each other. If your brand has an environmentally conscious image, then it must be seen through implementing equally eco-friendly policies. And so on and so forth.

These are just some of the ways that a good PR strategy can help your business improve on its image. The point is that being altruistic, amicable, and an overall fun brand to be around with has never been at the expense of one's competitiveness in the market.

Generating Great Publicity

Do you remember the phrase "There is no such thing as bad publicity"? Well, in the age of social media where every action you take is magnified and archived for future references, that is no longer true.

In fact, people can take what you said and done badly (no matter how noble the intentions are) and make a lot of fuss about it online. So what chances do you have in the market when your marketing strategies are intentionally designed to vilify, antagonize, and jeer people?

Bringing in the right kind of social media attraction is an essential strategy that you could take. And there are a few ways that you could go about doing that.

1. Media Relations

Personalities like bloggers, journalists, columnists, and reporters command a certain sphere of influence in the online world nowadays. This is why you need to extend effort to get on their good terms.

First, take the time to know how these people conduct themselves from their overall style to the topics that they often talk about. Then, you should reach out to them and convince them that having a relationship with your brand will prove to be beneficial on their part.

However, this is not to say that you want them to write biased puff pieces to push your credibility up. At best, these media folk can turn to you as an authority of sorts when it comes to certain social issues.

Also, having the media at your "side" tends to help soften a lot of fallout in case the market partially or completely rejects what you have to offer.

Let's look at Disney's case especially with their handling of the Star Wars brand. Because

George Lucas was able to establish goodwill with his target market for decades even before the rise of social media, the brand continues to command strong respect from authorities and is seen by many as a cultural icon.

This is why its Instagram campaigns are still generating a lot of engagement and why a lot of media folk are still willing to defend the franchise despite some current missteps. And such defense is even erected against some fans who feel that the brand is mishandled by the current management.

Fortunately, a lot of bloggers and media people frequent Instagram for a number of reasons. You can easily get a hold of them there or through their other social media channels.

2. Newsworthiness

Having friends in media is one thing. Generating enough buzz in that field is an entirely different challenge. What you may think is newsworthy content such as introducing new products or staff or even opening new branches may not exactly generate enough interest in the public.

Before releasing a story, you should consider how the public is going to react to that. You must ask yourself whether or not that story offers something that people will care about or find to be valuable. Instead of the usual announcements of new products/services/staff on Instagram, you can always use the platform to air out your brand's official stance on certain topics or show the world that your participating in charitable movements.

You can also become newsworthy by responding to breaking events. An official statement of sorts regarding certain incidents and how the brand stands with the community at large is often that effective in endearing your business to the public.

3. Damage Control

Although nobody should ever want to find themselves in having to deal with an emergency, the way you can handle such will have a strong impact than any planned publicity stunt. This is because an emergency forces you to handle things that you did not planned for, a sentiment that is shared by a lot of common folk today.

And in times of crisis, one good PR strategy is to immediately soften the fallout that could potentially occur from such event. Say, for example, a competitor leaked out competition about your company or a journalist wrote a scathing hit piece about your brand.

Naturally, outrage will be fanned which causes a lot of your customers to impulsively reject your products and services. So how is one supposed to react to all of that?

What any business should do is directly address the issue. Perhaps you could post something on Instagram that explains the rumors or denies them outright. Or, if the rumors are true, you can always issue a proper apology at the platform or through any of your major social media channels.

There is no assurance that the doubt implanted on your target markets is going to disappear. You might even have lost huge chunks of loyal customers for something that may be true or just blown out of proportion.

The point is that swift response is the key to proper damage control. The more you downplay things and not address legitimate concerns, the more damage that controversy can inflict to your brand.

To Conclude

Is public relations challenging? The answer is yes. There is so much effort that you have to make to establish goodwill and there is no assurance that people will ultimately see the brand in a positive light.

But is it worth it? The answer is still on the positive. Remember that being agreeable, amicable, and approachable as a business is never meant to dull one's competitive edge in the market. In fact, you can still go toe to toe with your more aggressive (and underhanded) competitors without becoming as cutthroat as them.

Public relations is all about maintaining that competitive edge and projecting such through solutions that benefit everyone, not just the company. If done right, you can establish a strong presence and command strong loyalty in your fanbase on the online world without having to step on other brands.

Chapter 9: Reaching the Online Marketing Plateau

Just like with any other field out there, online marketing can be like a ladder. As you learn new things and develop new strategies for platforms like Instagram, you slowly go through the ranks, get the hang of using what you learned, and proceed to the next big step on your venture.

But, as with any other field again, there comes a time when you reach a peak in marketing and, suddenly, there is no longer any growth or development. This is what is called as a plateau and it can be one of the most precarious places that any online marketer could find themselves in.

Why is this so? Because what follows after a plateau is a slope and, if you are not careful with your next steps, everything will go downhill from there.

Is there a way to get out of this lull? Yes, there is. It all boils down to what you can do to keep the momentum alive until the next big thing in marketing is announced.

What is the Plateau?

The "plateau" is actually a rather vague concept in marketing. You won't find it discussed thoroughly in an academic setting. Even industry experts have never even established a proper definition for it.

So what exactly is the plateau? To make things easier for you, here's a scenario.

Imagine that you are a fan of a certain movie franchise. After seeing the main character endure hardship after hardship in every past entry, you are now in the final movie where he is ready to face his ultimate adversary.

It is now the climax of the movie where both characters clash and the hero won. The ending is seen. The credits roll.

Suddenly, you are hit with this realization:

What Now?

This is a personal plateau for you and the same is true for marketers. Once every strategy has been learned, every trick of that channel mastered, and every trend identified, you feel that nothing can faze you now. There is no need for improvement anymore. Your place on social media is secured and your customer base is large and happy.

But, unlike natural plateaus, marketing plateaus are one of the most dangerous places to be in. In most cases, threats can come there in two forms.

1. Becoming Complacent

Picture yourself working so hard to master the features of Instagram while also making sure that your strategies there are well thought of. Luckily for you, they did which makes you happy.

Your success in one strategy gets you pumped up to create more strategies that eventually became successful themselves. But, with enough wins, you start losing that "fight" in you.

You and your brand feel that brand recognition is now enough to generate leads for the business so your staff start creating mediocre content. And, suddenly, a new standard in marketing pops up or Instagram made a massive change in their algorithms which affects businesses.

All of those strategies that you have learned and mastered are now deemed ineffective, bringing you back to square one. This is what exactly happened to those businesses at the dawn of the Internet age who did not bother to learn how to venture into the then-new market. By not learning how to do online marketing, they suddenly found out that all of their mastered skills and strategies were obsolete when social media started popping up.

2. Stagnating

Or what if you or your staff are not exactly reckless or that arrogant to think that your brand is untouchable. In fact, your business was paying attention closely to the changes in the market.

But, all of a sudden, your strategies are no longer yielding the engagements they once generated. Soon enough, your ventures in the online world start becoming expensive and ineffective for you.

This is what stagnation basically looks like. Your online venture, in its current form, has stopped performing well for your business. In most cases, the quality of your content has not changed. It is just that response for whatever your business is offering ranges from indifference to dislike.

Not addressing this problem has always proven to be a fatal move for marketers in the past. And it is important to note that online marketing is about to enter into a new age by the 2020s with a strong focus on personalized, intimate user experiences. Being at a plateau at this transition period will not do any business good.

What to Do, then?

The one thing that you have to understand with marketing plateaus is that everyone will eventually encounter them in their ventures. There will come a time when there will be no new developments on sight and a stagnation could be seen to last for a few months, depending on the platform.

And since plateaus are unavoidable, the best that any marketer could do is to make the most of their time there. Here's how:

1. Learn Where to Invest More

This strategy is hugely dependent on the assumption that your content had been warmly received in the past. To put it simply, if some of your content has not been generating the amount of engagement in Instagram but is otherwise good, then it is safe to assume that this kind of content needs a bit of an update.

This is a rather blunt strategy at this point since it requires you to do more than what you are currently doing. For instance, if you are posting on Instagram once per day, then increasing that number to 3 or 4 might do you favors. However, make sure that overall quality is not sacrificed with the increase in quantity.

2. Diversify

One other reason why reception for your content declines is the fact that you are offering the same thing over and over with little to no variation. Or perhaps you have been talking about the same topics over and over and people do get sick of hearing the same tune for months on end.

Even if the quality of your content can't be faulted, repetition does not encourage loyalty to the brand. Diversifying, however, keeps things fresh and entertaining which should drive up engagement for your business.

If you have been posting meme after meme on Instagram, for example, make sure that the next content is either a video or a quiz or a poll. The point is to never get stuck or be comfortable in doing the same thing again and again just to save effort on your part.

3. Look for a New Niche

If your current audience has been giving you the cold shoulder at worst or a lukewarm reception at best, then perhaps you could find better engagement from an entirely different market. Doing so opens your brand to new opportunities for marketing as well as new topics, issues, and strategies that you could learn and master.

To put it simply, venturing into new niches of the market not only helps in expanding the reach of your brand but it could also put you in a position to better hone your skills and diversify your content while in a rut.

Of course, the challenge here is to find that new niche. Catering to the same demographics might make it hard to find an alternative audience. To make this easier for you, try to watch what demographics your competitors are targeting or have yet to tap into. Either way, it is best not to limit one's reach to segments that the brand is most comfortable catering to.

4. Go Multimedia

If you had been providing too much image and text based content on Instagram, you run the risk of making people get tired of your content pretty quickly. Sure, pictures and text works great for retaining information but it does have the impact that videos and polls have.

Highly visual multimedia content tends to generate more engagement as it targets more senses while also adding a bit more diversity in your content lineup. And if you make that content interactive, you should drive engagements for your content to an even greater degree.

And if you think that going multimedia is going to run against the point of surviving a plateau, it doesn't. Memes, for example, are cheap to create but tend to be the most shareable media out there right now. You don't even have to change a lot just to keep things fresh. Of course, with memes, the trick is knowing when and how to deliver the punchline.

5. Consolidate Your Presence

Assuming that you are already implementing the ideas above, the next best thing is to try improving your online presence. For starters, you can revisit your defunct and often forgotten social media pages or even features in Instagram that you rarely use. You can even look at links in your content, bios, and pages to see if they still work in driving up traffic to your business.

Once you are assured that your presence is properly optimized, you can start on going back to your library of published content and retarget your niches, both old and new. Of course, there is the tried and tested method of collaborating with other creators and online influencers to attract even more audiences to your brand.

Surviving this plateau is going to be determined by your ability to adapt as well as mix and match effective marketing tools and strategies. Of course, it goes without saying that you must not lose sight of your overall goal as your business goes through the motions. Remember the priorities of the brand while trying out new things and the business should be able to stay afloat even if everything else in the market is stagnating.

Letting Go

One of the core rules in survival is to let go of the things that would weigh your down or prove to be unnecessary in the long term. If your resources are low and the chances of success are less than likely in your marketing ventures, there is even a risk to be had in insisting that your brand operates on the same scope or maintains the same number of channels and workforce.

This would be one of the hardest decisions you would have to make but it could be integral to your brand's survival in the online world. When downsizing your marketing operations, there are a few things that you need to consider.

1. Make a List

This is basic but essential to your survival of the Plateau. Make a list of all the channels currently employed by the brand, the tools at your disposal, and the strategies and campaigns that you are currently running. This is where analytics would also come into play as you need to know how your channels are performing in terms of engagement, web traffic, and search results page visibility.

Then, slowly arrange these channels and strategies according to how well they are performing. With a clearly set distinction between channels and campaigns that are working the best and the least, you will have a better idea as to which of them you should terminate.

2. Remain as Objective as Possible

Cleaning house can be hard. There might be campaigns or strategies that you and your staff have a sentimental connection to or there might be channels where you made your first steps in online marketing.

When you have to confront the fact that some things have to be let go, you should maintain an objective mindset. Try to establish the most logical reason why you are scrapping of this project so you at the very least don't devalue the efforts everybody has poured into it. Make sure that everybody else in the team knows why this is happening so they could shift their efforts elsewhere. And speaking of elsewhere...

3. Take a Hit

Aside from projects and strategies, there is also the chance that you would have to let go of some key people on your staff. At this point, you must prove to your people that this downsizing is also going to affect your business and yourself.

For example, if you are going to let go of a few people, then at the very least try to make them see that you are hurting economically. A pay cut here or reduced bonuses (or better yet, none at all) for you can do a lot in projecting solidarity with your team. And by assuring them that whatever you do will ultimately help the business in the long run, there is at the least the chance that morale for your staff is not severely hurt.

To Conclude

A plateau is not exactly the easiest thing to pass through for any marketing venture. More often than not, your brand will not be the same after passing here provided, of course, that you managed to survive through the ordeal.

However, what you have to understand is that plateaus are unavoidable things in marketing. If you don't hit one on your marketing, then good for you since you might be one of the lucky few out there.

If you do stumble on your own marketing campaign plateau, you must be able to find a creative workaround for your current predicament. This way, your stay there would be a bit more manageable.

Conclusion

After learning everything that you could ever possibly want to know on how to pull off a marketing campaign on Instagram, there is still one question that you need to answer:

Is marketing on Instagram all worth it?

This does not ask if the platform is the right fit for your business as that is something that you should answer yourself. What it does ask, however, is if there is a point to even trying to venture into Instagram.

When it comes to Instagram, there are always 4 points that you have to consider in determining if the platform is the right channel to do your marketing in.

1. Stories Matter now More than Ever

The launch of Instagram stories and other similar features in social media sites have proved one thing for marketers: you can no longer sell anything online just with pretty pictures or quotable text.

Stories have a highly interactive and multimedia nature in them which means that they can be consumed in various ways (even ways that you did not plan for) and encourage people to engage with the, driving traffic up to a considerable degree. And if people are engaged, they retain information at a far better rate.

And, of course, stories make your marketing content all the more personal and we have discussed thoroughly as to how people respond well if you engage with them on a personal, intimate level.

2. Everyone Is Into Collaborating

Influencers have played a hugely vital role in marketing during the latter half of the 2010s and their influence could not be felt more than in the Instagram community. Their ability to command a following while also compelling the same to do things that they ask for is something that modern-day marketers would wish they have right now.

But here is the thing that you need to understand about Influencers. In order for them to effectively become an ambassador of the brand, you have to successfully win them over as a customer themselves. In other words, they themselves must come to the conclusion that whatever you offer works so they could tell others the same.

Looking for the right influencer does pose some challenges for brands nowadays but rest assured that there is always the right influencer for any kind of business.

3. E-Commerce is the Key to Conversion

Online marketing in the last few years of the 2010s has seemingly shifted to a policy of "Show, Don't Tell". What this simply means is that they are slowly migrating a portion of their sales processes from their main web page to the wherever platform they do their marketing in and Instagram is no different with its inclusion of the shopping feature.

The reason for this is quite simple: conversation rates tend to speed up even more if the audience member does not have to sift through multiple websites just to complete a deal. The least likely they have to hop from page to page just to get what they want, the easier it will be to make them part with their hard-earned cash.

We are in a day and where one's own image can be made and unmade with just one status update. Customers that insist on doing things on a purely marketing-focused approach tend to find it hard to make a connection with their target markets who want something more.

In Instagram, businesses should offer more than their usual products and services. They should be selling lifestyles, ideas, and relationships as this is what makes people gravitate towards the site. And it is good to know that you can adapt to the culture of the site without having to forego what makes your brand unique or, on technical terms, what it is trying to do with its online marketing campaigns.

So, should you be on Instagram at all? The answer is a definite 'yes'. By creating campaigns that speaks to your audience on a personal level while still ticking the usual marketing check boxes, you should find a rather warm reception for whatever you have to offer to the site.

Thank you for taking the time and effort to go through every page of this book. Now that you have learned all that is to know about pulling off an effective marketing campaign on Instagram, all that is left to do is to apply everything that you have mastered.

Good Luck!

Thank you

Before you go, I just wanted to say thank you for purchasing my book.

You could have picked from dozens of other books on the same topic but you took a chance and chose this one.

So, a HUGE thanks to you for getting this book and for reading all the way to the end.

Now I wanted to ask you for a small favor. ***Could you please consider posting a review on the platform? Reviews are one of the easiest ways to support the work of independent authors.***

This feedback will help me continue to write the type of books that will help you get the results you want. So if you enjoyed it, please let me know!

Lastly, don't forget to grab a copy of your Free Bonuses *"**The Fastest Way to Make Money with Affiliate Marketing**" and "**Top 10 Affiliate Offers to Promote**".*
Just go to the link below.
https://theartofmastery.com/chandler-free-gift

Printed in Great Britain
by Amazon